HD
9506
.U63
A17153
1991

Peterson, Richard H.

The bonanza kings.

$10.95

BAKER & TAYLOR BOOKS

The
Bonanza Kings

THE SOCIAL ORIGINS AND BUSINESS BEHAVIOR OF WESTERN MINING ENTREPRENEURS, 1870–1900

Richard H. Peterson

UNIVERSITY OF OKLAHOMA PRESS
NORMAN AND LONDON

For my parents,
Bill and Dorothy

HD
9506
.U63
A17153
1991

Cover design by Sue Hollingsworth

Library of Congress Cataloging-in-Publication Data

Peterson, Richard H.
   The bonanza kings : the social origins and business behavior of
western mining entrepreneurs, 1870–1900 / Richard H. Peterson.
     p.   cm.
   Includes bibliographical references and index.
   ISBN 0-8061-2389-3 (pbk.)
   1. Mineral industries—West (U.S.)—Biography. 2. Industrialists–
United States—Biography. 3. Mineral industries—West (U.S.)—
History—19th century. 4. West (U.S.)—Social conditions.
I. Title.
HD9506.U63A17153
338.2′092′273—dc20
[B]
                              91-50311
                                    CIP

Published by the University of Oklahoma Press, Norman, Publishing Division of the University. Copyright © 1971, 1977 by
the University of Nebraska Press; assigned January 31, 1990,
to Richard H. Peterson. New edition copyright © 1991 by Richard H. Peterson. All rights reserved. Manufactured in the
U.S.A. First printing of the University of Oklahoma Press edition, 1991.

CONTENTS

TABLES

PREFACE TO THE PAPERBACK EDITION

SINCE THIS BOOK was first published in 1977, there has been a recent interest in the social history of the western mining frontier and industry. Although no work has appeared, to the best of my knowledge, to alter my conclusions about entrepreneurial social mobility or my basic thesis, various monographs analyzing the saloon, demography, women, prostitutes, and vigilantes exemplify the historiographical trend toward a "new social history" of the mining West. For example, Elliott West, *The Saloon on the Rocky Mountain Mining Frontier* (Lincoln: University of Nebraska Press, 1979) utilizes qualitative and quantitative data to determine the structure, function, and evolution of saloons and the personal characteristics of saloon keepers. Ralph Mann, *After the Gold Rush: Society in Grass Valley and Nevada City, California, 1849– 1870* (Stanford: Stanford University Press, 1982) discusses such demographic factors as age, gender, education, occupation, race, ethnicity, marital status, property ownership, and other variables to recreate the social structure and values of two diverse communities dependent on mining. An excellent case study of how prostitution was integrated into the community life and social institutions of the Comstock Lode, especially in the 1870s, is Marion Goldman, *Gold Diggers and Silver Miners: Prostitution and Social Life on the Comstock Lode* (Ann Arbor: University of Michigan Press, 1981). Paula Petrik, *No Step Backward: Women and Family on the Rocky Mountain Mining Frontier, Helena, Montana,*

1865–1900 (Seattle: University of Washington Press, 1987) is a well-balanced community study, collective biography, and statistical portrait of the town's female residents. The familiar topic of frontier violence has found a revisionist comparative treatment in Robert Senkewicz, *Vigilantes in Gold Rush San Francisco* (Stanford: Stanford University Press, 1985), which essentially attributes vigilante activity of the 1850s to the economic and political frustrations of local businessmen. Other works on the social history of the mining frontier could be cited, but these aptly illustrate the increasing diversity and quality of scholarship.

At the same time, more traditional studies have appeared in the past thirteen years that illuminate mining as an industry. Utilizing some of the investors who appear in this book, Joseph King wrote a solid account of the impact and political implications of primarily eastern investment capital on Colorado mining in *A Mine to Make a Mine: Financing the Colorado Mining Industry, 1859–1902* (College Station: Texas A&M University Press, 1977). Further enlightenment on Colorado mining is provided by James E. Fell, Jr., *Ores to Metals: The Rocky Mountain Smelting Industry* (Lincoln: University of Nebraska Press, 1979), which demonstrates the critical importance of smelters to the success of mine production and the crucial role of technology in the industry. Michael Malone, *The Battle for Butte: Mining and Politics on the Northern Frontier, 1864–1906* (Seattle: University of Washington Press, 1981) is a community study of Butte and an update of C. B. Glasscock's older work (cited in the bibliography) regarding the economic and political feud involving William Clark, Marcus Daly, and Augustus Heinze.

The working class has been well served by several good books. Mark Wyman, *Hard Rock Epic: Western Miners and the Industrial Revolution, 1860–1910* (Berkeley: University of California Press, 1979) examines the various responses and problems of hard-rock miners as they struggled to adjust to industrialization. Ronald Brown, *Hard-Rock Miners: The Intermountain West, 1860–1920* (College Station: Texas A&M University Press, 1979) takes an ambitious look at the typically harsh occupational problems of such men as well as the lighter recreational side of their lives. Other labor studies have emphasized the violent or radical aspect of mining reminiscent of Vernon H. Jensen's earlier overview, *Heritage of Conflict* (in the bibliography). Jerry Calvert, *The Gibraltar: Socialism and Labor in Butte, Montana, 1895–1920* (Seattle: University of Washington Press, 1988) probes the role of radical unionism and socialism in Butte politics, especially given the dynamiting of the Butte Miners' Union Hall in 1914. This work should be used in conjunction with David Emmons, *The Butte Irish: Class and Ethnicity in an American Mining Town, 1875–1925* (Champaign: University of Illinois Press, 1989), which examines Butte's large and aggressive population of Irish immigrants and their position in the community, the miners' union, and the largest mining companies.

The destructive environmental impact of mining and the ensuing public and political response have been surveyed objectively in Duane A. Smith, *Mining America: The Industry and the Environment, 1800–1980* Lawrence: University Press of Kansas, 1987). The paperback reprint of Smith's *Horace Tabor: His Life and the Legend* (Niwot: University Press of Colorado, 1989) suggests that there still is interest in the individual entrepreneurs who created an industry out of a wilderness. Useful but less important books on mining entrepreneurial history include the following: John Fahey, *The Days of the Hercules* (Moscow: University Press of Idaho, 1978); Diane M. T. North, *Samuel Peter Heintzelman and the Sonora Exploring and Mining Company* (Tucson: University of Arizona Press, 1980); and Donald Abbe, *Austin and the Reese*

River Mining District: Nevada's Forgotten Frontier (Reno: University of Nevada Press, 1985). Clark Spence, *The Conrey Placer Mining Company: A Pioneer Gold-Dredging Enterprise in Montana, 1897–1922* (Helena: Montana Historical Society Press, 1989) explores a relatively untouched dimension of an industry traditionally studied from the perspective of lode or quartz mining.

These and other books update and supplement my original analysis of how the bonanza kings succeeded in the precious and non-precious metal-mining industries by examining the various factors of production and individuals necessary to accumulate vast fortunes. Despite the continuing interest in the history of ghost towns and mining camps of the California gold rush, exemplified by the popularity and quality of J. S. Holliday, *The World Rushed In: The California Gold Rush Experience* (New York: Simon and Schuster, 1981), the sophisticated industrialist rather than the primitive prospector deserves most of the credit for developing the economic and community base of the mining frontier. Yet, the prospector, prostitute, saloon keeper, vigilante, mine worker, engineer, finance capitalist, and others all played a part in weaving the colorful, but often flawed, human tapestry of the great western mining lottery.

RICHARD H. PETERSON

San Diego State University

PREFACE TO THE FIRST EDITION

THE MINING FRONTIER of the trans-Mississippi West has been traditionally and popularly associated with the colorful prospector, pan in hand or pick poised for that elusive lucky strike. Tirelessly chasing the rumor of discovery from camp to camp, he became a familiar figure on the frontier, opening and publicizing mining districts for further development. However, as the surface placers declined and the technological and capital demands of mining increased, he retired into romantic oblivion until resurrected by the mass media and western history buffs. Returning to the "States," finding other occupations in the West, or joining the corporate mining labor force, he gave way to the industrial mining entrepreneur—the bonanza king who became a more enduring and creative force in the West.

In the Introduction to *The Cattle Kings*, Lewis Atherton recognized the need to examine this type of entrepreneur: "It seems to me that the time has come to consider the dominant personalities on the various frontiers in terms of group characteristics."[1] Accordingly, I have attempted to study the social origins and business behavior of fifty prominent owners of mines, mills, and/ or smelters in the precious and related nonprecious metals mining industry of the trans-Mississippi West during approximately the last thirty years of the nineteenth century.

Classification as a bonanza king is based on several criteria, but primarily on financial success. Thirty-six of the fifty mining businessmen or members of their immediate families were regarded as millionaires according to surveys conducted by the *New York Tribune* in 1892 and the *New York World* in 1902.[2] Undoubtedly, many of them held high, if not the highest, positions in the largest mining companies as defined by capitalization or production. Their business leadership was comparable to that of the men who dominated the fields of steel, oil, or railroads.

Most of the mining entrepreneurs were also chosen because they appeared in the *Dictionary of American Biography,* the *National Cyclopedia of American Biography,* or both. Each series listed the country's most prominent or successful businessmen. In a collective study of 1,464 business leaders born between 1570 and 1879, C. Wright Mills made his selections from the *DAB*, reasoning that the *Dictionary* "forms a convenient point of departure for an over-all view of the social characteristics of eminent American businessmen."[3] Of the fifty mining magnates, thirty-two were the subjects of biographical essays in either the *DAB* or the *NCAB*. Some appeared in both series.

Nonabsentee ownership provided an additional criterion for selection. No attempt was made to eliminate those who became nonabsentee owners after mining properties had matured. Nonetheless, most of the men chosen had joined the early rushes to the major mining frontiers and districts and had stayed on to mature with their properties. Their early arrival in the West helps explain their success. These westerners can be contrasted with such eastern mining financiers as Henry H. Rogers of the Amalgamated Copper Company or Daniel Guggenheim of the American Smelting and Refining Company, who operated their enterprises from a distance and usually invested in western mining after it had become heavily industrialized.

In the interest of balanced regional representation, an attempt was made to select moguls from nearly all of the western mining frontiers and the most productive mining districts. Although these bonanza kings are identified with their major fields of investment or operation in the appendix, they are not differentiated specifically by region in the other tables. In view of the multiple regional investments of most mining entrepreneurs in this study, such a differentiation would be misleading if not somewhat unrepresentative.

Considerations of time as well as place helped to determine the sample. The period, 1870–1900, was singled out for special attention. Despite the continuing instability of frontier social and economic conditions, this era saw western mining mature into a technologically sophisticated industry surrounded by an increasingly stable population base and labor force. In particular, the wandering prospector had given way to the resident wage-earning miner. On the whole, the subjects of the study were most productive and most prominent during these years, although their mining careers often had begun before 1870 and for some had continued after the turn of the century. Indications of career length and success can be derived roughly from the lifetime statistics available in the appendix.

By 1900 or shortly thereafter, the industry had undergone structural changes in the form of increased corporate consolidation and eastern financial domination. Even before 1900, mining was becoming a part of the national economy rather than continuing to be primarily an isolated western endeavor.[4] Such heavily capitalized national corporations as the American Smelting and Refining Company, Phelps Dodge Corporation, and the Amalgamated Copper Company were beginning to dominate the industry as completely as the western bonanza kings previously had controlled local mining districts. The turn of the century thus seems appropriate as a terminal date for the selection of leading western mining careers. From a practical standpoint, readily available biographical information also influenced selection of the sample.[5] Although the book is intended largely as a synthesis of secondary sources, unpublished primary sources were not neglected. Personal and business papers were utilized for some of the entrepreneurs. The Thomas F. Walsh Family Papers in the Library of Congress, the Jesse Knight Family Papers in the Brigham Young University Archives, the Horace A. W. Tabor Papers in the State Historical Society of Colorado, and the Simeon G. Reed Papers at Reed College were typical of those consulted. Unpublished biographical theses and dissertations could be found for seven of the men, and twenty-two entrepreneurs were subjects of published biographies, autobiographies, memoirs, and magazine articles. In sum, for the purposes of this study a bonanza king is generally defined as a wealthy, western owner of various late nineteenth-century mining and related enterprises, who was important enough to be included in the contemporary biographical encyclopedias or to be remembered by modern historians.

The study is concerned primarily with the causes of economic success. Therefore, it seeks to determine how mining entrepreneurs secured and managed property, labor, capital, and technology in order to succeed. At least for the fifty mining leaders in this work, the business behavior described led to success. That is not to preclude the possibility that other business strategies would have been similarly rewarded. It is hoped that a behavioral approach will increase our understanding of the process of western economic development.

It was not possible to analyze systematically or quantitatively the business behavior of the mining entrepreneurs. Complete systematic information on the managerial motives and policies of fifty men was unavailable. Many mining moguls no doubt sought to keep this information confidential. Given the scarcity of collections of manuscript business papers and the uneven group of sources with which I had to work, my analysis of business behavior had to be somewhat selective and impressionistic or it could not have been attempted at all.

The study also seeks to discover the character of success in the mining industry. In short, did the business operations of the fifty bonanza kings conform to the stereotypes that have been popularly associated with the prospector and the mining frontier, such as individualism, self-sufficiency, and violence? The question should help the student of the frontier distinguish myth from reality.

I have not limited my questions to business behavior or to the West. The book is intended to shed some light on the controversial problem of whether the West differed significantly from the rest of the nation. Accordingly, I have compared quantitatively the social origins of western mining leaders with those of national (mostly eastern) entrepreneurial elites. The approach permits a partial reexamination of the frontier thesis advocated by Frederick Jackson Turner.

In researching the careers of fifty men, I have drawn heavily on the resources and good will of many individuals and institutions. Special thanks must be extended to the staffs of the Inter-library Loan Department of the University of California at Davis, the Bancroft Library on the Berkeley campus of the University of California, the California Historical Society, the Sutro Branch of the California State Library, the Reed College Library, the Utah State Historical Society, the Brigham Young University Archives, the State Historical Society of Colorado, the National Archives, and the Manuscript Division of the Library of Congress.

I am especially indebted to Dr. W. Turrentine Jackson
of the University of California at Davis. The idea for the
study was his, and he gave generously of his immense
knowledge of western mining history during the preparation of the book. Also, at the Davis campus, Dr.
Morgan B. Sherwod and Dr. David Brody patiently contributed their time and talent to ensure that the study
realized its potential. Dr. Norris Hundley of the University of California at Los Angeles and the able editorial referees of the *Pacific Historical Review* helped me
refine the argument in the initial chapter. Through the
assistance of Dr. James B. Allen of Brigham Young
University, I gained access to the Jesse Knight Papers. A
Faculty Summer Fellowship from Indiana University
provided the opportunity to complete the research and
writing of the study. I would also like to thank my wife,
Nora, and daughter, Nina, for their patience and in-
dulgence. They lost a husband and father temporarily
but gained a historian. I am not sure that the exchange
was fair to them. Obviously, I assume full responsibility
for all errors.

RICHARD H. PETERSON

ONE

SOCIAL MOBILITY ON THE MINING FRONTIER

As FREDERICK JACKSON TURNER pondered the 1890 announcement of the United States Bureau of the Census that the frontier had closed, he found reason to recall America's frontier heritage: "Not the constitution, but free land and an abundance of natural resources open to a fit people, made the democratic type of society in America. . . . These free lands promoted individualism, economic equality, freedom to rise, democracy."[1] Turner's contention that the frontier encouraged rapid upward social mobility was more a product of logic and imagination than of empirical evidence. Recently, historians using computerized and other quantitative techniques have subjected this aspect of the frontier thesis to close, systematic scrutiny. Although promising, the results have been inconclusive. In fact, there is a growing debate between those who find evidence to support Turner and those who find the degree of social escalation on the frontier not so great as was formerly supposed. Evidence of an open and upwardly mobile frontier society has been provided by scholars who have examined selected aspects of the American experience: the tendency of immigrants to Maryland in the seventeenth century to claim the rank of gentleman upon arrival, despite a somewhat lower standing previously in England; the relatively even distribution of wealth in Dedham, Massachusetts, between 1636 and 1736; the excellent economic opportunities for first- and second-generation settlers in western Connecticut before the American

Revolution; the frequency of marriage between members of slaveholding and nonslaveholding families in five Alabama counties during the 1850s; and the rapid rise of non-English-speaking Europeans from farm laborer to farm owner in late nineteenth-century Trempealeau County, Wisconsin.[2]

Scholars also have found reason to question or to qualify Turner's argument in behalf of frontier social mobility. The high rates of population turnover in Grass Valley and Nevada City, California, between 1850 and 1856, in Roseburg, Oregon, in the 1860s, and in Grant County, Wisconsin, between 1885 and 1895 suggest limited or dwindling opportunities for social advancement. Given a direct relationship between length of residence and economic condition, the unsuccessful were more likely to leave than the successful. In certain pioneer communities and counties, the median age of property holders was the mid-thirties and wealth was concentrated in an elite group. For example, in Manistee County, Michigan, a typical timber frontier region in 1860, the wealthiest 10 percent of the population held 38 percent of all the property. By 1880, some 20 percent of Roseburg's population controlled 80 percent of the community wealth. Such ethnic groups as the Irish and Chinese in Grass Valley and Nevada City in the decade after the gold rush were usually denied access to community wealth and relegated to inferior positions in the social structure. This demographic picture is hardly consistent with an open frontier society.[3]

Further, some scholars argue that the eastern industrial city was as likely to generate vertical social mobility as the frontier farm or pioneer county. For example, Stephan Thernstrom contends that advancement opportunities for those at the bottom of the social ladder in Newburyport, Massachusetts, and Trempealeau County, Wisconsin, were not radically different during the period

1850–80. Thernstrom's examination of Boston from 1880 to 1970 indicates that about a third of the youths from working-class families ended their careers in middle-class jobs, while downward mobility for middle-class youths occurred much less frequently than blue-collar climbing.[4] The Boston study indicates that it is at least possible that the young man on the make found greater opportunities in the eastern city than on the western frontier.

In view of conflicting evidence and interpretations, only partial answers have been supplied to the basic question of whether the frontier created an opportunity for vertical mobility as Turner argued. Additional insight into the problem can be achieved by examining the social origins of frontier elites, in this case, leading entrepreneurs in the precious and related nonprecious metals mining industry of the trans-Mississippi West.[5]

A comparison with similarly influential and successful entrepreneurs of the older, more settled areas of the nation should disclose whether the frontier, or the West, was as unique as Turner contended. Therefore, references will be made to two studies of the recruitment of national, mostly eastern, business elites, one by Frances Gregory and Irene Neu, the other by William Miller.[6] Although based on a much more extensive sample than mine, these investigations define categories for comparison and consider leading capitalists of the 1870s and the decade 1901–10—dates near the beginning and terminal points, respectively, of this study. Miller primarily studied leading business bureaucrats of the later decade. Gregory and Neu largely examined less bureaucratic entrepreneurs and organizers of family-owned companies. Most of the fifty mining magnates studied here appear to have been original organizers of their own companies as well as officeholders in these companies.

Of the fifty entrepreneurs, 35 (70 percent) were native

Americans, while 15 (30 percent) were foreign born. A different picture emerges when these statistics are compared with those for eastern capitalists. Of the 187 business executives whose birthplaces are known, Miller found that only 18, or less than 10 percent, were born abroad. For the industrial elite of the 1870s, Gregory and Neu made similar findings; only 10 percent of the nearly 250 leaders examined could be classified as foreign born.[7]

Dissimilarities between western and eastern elites also appear when one considers the economic status of the immigrant. Popular belief sometimes has associated poor immigrants, such as Andrew Carnegie, with economic success. According to recent scholarship, foreign-born capitalists of the 1870s and the early twentieth century usually had not known economic hardship in their early lives. More often, they had grown up in substantial middle-class or comfortable upper-class surroundings. The same cannot be said for their counterparts on the mining frontier. Of the fifteen immigrant bonanza kings, nine had experienced poverty in their youth; the remainder came from middle-class backgrounds. Joseph and Matthew Walker, mid-century English immigrants who became prominent in Utah mining, took their first jobs after the untimely death of their father and the loss of the family fortune. Dennis Sheedy, who emigrated to the United States from England in 1847, had to overcome similar disadvantages. Forced to go to work before his teens, he had become one of Colorado's major smelting and refining entrepreneurs by the turn of the century.[8] Apparently, the relatively poor immigrant had a somewhat better chance of becoming a leading industrialist on the mining frontier than in the more established sections of the country.

National and ethnic origins, however, could sometimes prove an obstacle to success. Of the fifteen alien mining moguls, seven were born in Ireland, four in England, and two in Canada. The remaining two were of German or Dutch birth. In short, immigrants from the British Empire were significantly represented among the elites. Notably absent from the ranks of leading mining capitalists were the French, Latin Americans, Chinese, and Pacific islanders, although all of these groups were represented on the mining frontier. Since many of these foreigners, especially the Latin Americans, were ex-

TABLE 1
WESTERN MINING LEADERS BY PATERNAL
FAMILY'S ORIGIN

Family Origin*	My Totals (1870–1900) (%)	Gregory/Neu Totals (1870–79) (%)	Miller Totals (1901–10) (%)
England and Wales	48	71	53
Ireland	28	11	14
Scotland	7	7	7
Canada	5	2	3
Other British Empire Countries	0	0	5
British Empire	88	91	82
Germany	7	4	12
Other Countries	5	5	6
Total Cases† (= 100%)	42	175	162

*If the business leader was the first in his family to settle in America, the data refer to the country in which he was born. In any case, the statistics identify the last country before settlement in America. In this and succeeding tables, the clarifications appearing in the notes are those used by William Miller and Frances Gregory and Irene Neu, except where the backgrounds of mining leaders demanded additional clarification or qualification.

†In this and all other tables where cases are fewer than fifty, the difference indicates the number of men about whom information was unavailable.

perienced miners, ignorance of mining technology fails to explain their inability to become bonanza kings. Cultural and language barriers partially account for their lack of achievement, but discrimination by the native Americans is a more plausible explanation.[9] This can be seen more readily when the national origins of the native and foreign bonanza kings are considered together. As table 1 indicates, comparison with the findings of Gregory and Neu and Miller reveals a near uniformity of descent among entrepreneurial elites.

During the last quarter of the nineteenth century, men of British origins, whether in the mining West or the industrially diverse East, found opportunities for outstanding economic achievement. Such men were represented in the upper echelons of American business far out of proportion to their representation in the population generally.[10] Their success is, perhaps, not surprising in a country where a British cultural heritage and knowledge of the English language could work to one's economic advantage. Nonetheless, both the West and the nation at large appear to have been similarly unyielding in granting equality of economic opportunity to members of racial and ethnic minority groups.

An examination of business leaders by national ancestry raises a related question. Were the several sections of this country as disproportionately represented among mining leaders as certain nations? The percentages to the right of the columns in table 2 indicate that the eastern United States was the leading producer of both western mining and national business elites. Among the former, however, the several sections of the country found a more balanced representation. Although comparative statistics on the regional origins of the general population in the West and in the East are needed before conclusions can be drawn, it would appear that native-

TABLE 2
AMERICAN-BORN WESTERN MINING LEADERS
BY REGION OF BIRTHPLACE

Birthplace*	My Totals (1870–1900) (%)	Gregory/Neu Totals (1870–79) (%)	Miller Totals (1901–10) (%)
New England	20 ⎫	57 ⎫	20 ⎫
	⎬ 54	⎬ 89	⎬ 61
Middle Atlantic	34 ⎭	32 ⎭	41 ⎭
East North Central	17	5	24
South	23	3	10
West	6	1	5
U.S.,unspecified	0	2	0
Total Cases (= 100%)	35	222	169

*These are census regions. Combined in "South" are south Atlantic, south central, west south central; in "West" are west north central, mountain, Pacific. "East North Central" is largely equivalent to the Old Northwest Territory. The original figures of Gregory and Neu and Miller included the foreign and native born. These figures have been adjusted to include only the native born.

born bonanza kings could more convincingly claim a national identity than could their capitalist counterparts in predominantly eastern companies.

The foregoing discussion shows that the ethnic, national, and regional backgrounds of the western mining entrepreneurs are both similar to and different from those of the national business elites. For example, the bonanza kings, like their eastern counterparts, were predominantly of British ancestry. An examination of success among immigrants reveals that the bonanza kings were unlike leading eastern capitalists in one important respect: early poverty did not deter, though it may have delayed, their ultimate economic achievement. Evidence of social mobility among immigrant bonanza kings raises the question for bonanza kings in general.

The occupations of the fathers of western mining magnates provide, perhaps, the most telling evidence of social mobility. Those fathers designated as businessmen usually found employment in merchandising or manufacturing. Others in this category held such disparate jobs as bank manager, gristmill operator, stonemason, and tannery owner. Professionals were generally either lawyers or clergymen. "Public official" included professional politicians and lawyers who were primarily public servants. These occupational categories and those which are self-explanatory are compared for western and eastern capitalists in table 3. By equating the farm with

TABLE 3
WESTERN MINING LEADERS
BY FATHER'S OCCUPATION

Occupation*	My Totals (1870–1900) (%)	Gregory/Neu Totals (1870–79) (%)	Miller Totals (1901–10) (%)
Businessman	41	51	55
Professional	10	13	22
Farmer	39	25	14
Public Official	5	3	7
Worker	5	8	2
Total Cases (= 100%)	41	194	167

*Some fathers engaged in more than one occupation. The one selected was dominant in the period in which each leader was reared. Miller did not explain what was meant by *dominant*. As used here the term indicates length of service in, rather than economic return from, a specific occupation. If the father of a mining leader died when his son was very young, the occupation prior to his death is recorded.

rural surroundings, it is obvious that the bonanza king more closely conforms to the popular country boy success stories of Horatio Alger than does his eastern counterpart, who often came from an urban professional or business-bred background.[11]

These crude occupational categories can be used to determine social status and class membership. For many future bonanza kings life on a mid-century farm was harsh and demanding. As a young boy in Utah, Jesse Knight, a prominent silver miner, "knew nothing much but hardships such as herding cows barefooted, gathering pigweeds and sego roots as a help toward the family's meager food supply. His clothing consisted of coarse homespun cloth, sacks and madeover clothes of all kinds."[12] Obviously, not all mining magnates lived on small, subsistence-level farms. Some farmers, such as the father of James B. Grant of Colorado smelting and refining fame, held estates or large areas of plantation land. However, *farmer* usually designated a person who owned a small family-operated farm and who had income and status more nearly like those of the lower class than those of the middle class. According to Miller's criteria, wealth or political eminence, often associated with the big businessman or professional, defined the upper-class. James B. Haggin, whose partnership with George Hearst yielded success in various mining fields, was born into this group. Haggin's father was a wealthy Kentucky lawyer able to give his son a college education and postgraduate legal training.[13] Again according to Miller's criteria, those in between—including some businessmen with no special claims to wealth or power or such professionals as the average clergyman or lawyer—were regarded as members of the middle class. Besides occupational categories, the ability of the father to give his son an education was considered in computing class origins, especially when the economic standing of the father was unknown. A common school education helped to identify the lower class, while higher education gave evidence of an upper-class background. The terms "class" and "status" were used cautiously in table 4 since precise definitions are impossible to give. However, the primary reason for using such terminology is not to achieve absolute precision, but to determine the relative difference between social mobility in the West and in the rest of the nation.

TABLE 4
WESTERN MINING LEADERS
BY FAMILY STATUS OR CLASS

Status/Class	My Totals (1870–1900) (%)	Miller Totals (1901–10) (%)
Upper	20	50
Middle	44	45
Lower	36	5
Total Cases (= 100%)	45	179

Ninety-five percent of the leading American capitalists of the early twentieth century were of upper or middle-class origins. According to Gregory and Neu, the industrial elite of the 1870s came from similar backgrounds:

> Precise calculations of class or status do not seem feasible, but every effort to take all known factors into account reemphasizes the general impression that most—perhaps 90 per cent—of the industrial leaders in our group were reared in a middle or upper class milieu.[14]

Eighty percent of the bonanza kings were born into lower- or middle-class families. Thus, in comparison with the older, more established sections of the nation, the mining frontier was more democratic. A poor, uneducated country boy like Knight or Marcus Daly, who became a Montana copper king, had a better chance for outstanding business success in the West than in the East.

The rate of social ascent on the mining frontier becomes more dramatic when one looks beyond table 4 into the personal backgrounds of individual mining leaders. Some renounced the assets of a prosperous, well-connected family for the opportunity to make it on their own. David Moffat, a Colorado railroad and mining mogul classified among the upper-class on the basis of his family's economic and political standing, went to work when only twelve years old after completing common school, even though his father could have provided him with a college education. Other bonanza kings, ranked in the middle class because of their fathers' occupations, were forced into economic independence at an early age by the untimely death of the family provider. The Walker brothers of Utah have already been cited. Captain Joseph R. DeLamar, who had a profitable mining career in Colorado, Idaho, and Utah, overcame such a handicap. His father, a relatively prosperous Dutch bank manager, died when DeLamar was six years old, causing Joseph to seek a life at sea when only a boy.[15] Thus, the mining magnates experienced even greater social mobility than is indicated by table 4.

The findings in table 5 suggest that before achieving success the western entrepreneurs had to overcome more serious educational limitations than their eastern capitalist counterparts. Obviously, we need to know the educational levels attained by the general population in the West and in the East before claiming greater opportunity for the less educated on the frontier. Nevertheless, the college educated entrepreneur apparently was more common in the older areas of the nation than on the

TABLE 5
WESTERN MINING LEADERS
BY HIGHEST EDUCATIONAL LEVEL ATTAINED

Education*	My Totals (1870–1900) (%)	Gregory/Neu Totals (1870–79) (%)	Miller Totals (1901–10) (%)
Grammar School	45	30	22
High School	34	33	37
College	21	37	41
Total Cases (= 100%)	47	183	183

*The many types of older schools have been reduced to modern terminology. Included in "grammar schools" are institutions called by that name, as well as district, public, common, and similar schools. In "high school" are included academies and other institutions of similar rank. Counted among grammar school boys are those who had little or no formal education as well as graduates; among high school boys, all those who attended whether graduates or not. The same rule applies to college men. In some cases individuals returned to school after having assumed their first regular job. The statistics above refer to the educational level reached before going to work for the first time.

frontier, where most mining moguls could claim only a common school education.

Given the limited education of most bonanza kings, one would expect an early entry into the work force. Table 6 shows that almost half of the mining leaders for whom data are available had begun to earn a living by the time they were fifteen. In contrast, less than one-quarter of the national business elites of the 1870s and the early twentieth century had begun work when they were younger than sixteen. Generally, western mining magnates did not enjoy the late business start of their capitalist counterparts east of the Mississippi.

TABLE 6
WESTERN MINING LEADERS
BY AGE ON GOING TO WORK

Age*	My Totals (1870–1900) (%)	Gregory/Neu Totals (1870–79) (%)	Miller Totals (1901–10) (%)
15 or under	40	23	20
16–18	33	32	35
19 and over	27	45	45
Total Cases (= 100%)	45	176	179

*Age on taking first regular business, professional, or other job, except work on father's or other relative's farm, after leaving school.

Thus, the typical western bonanza king of the late nineteenth century was native born and of British ancestry. He had overcome a limited education and the lower- or middle-class environment of the family farm or small business and had risen to success. Although English by national origin and American by birth, the leading national, or predominantly eastern, capitalist of the same era demands a different description:

> He was rather born and bred in an atmosphere in which business and a relatively high social standing were intimately associated with his family life. Only at about eighteen did he take his first regular job, prepared to rise from it, moreover, not by a rigorous apprenticeship begun when he was virtually a child, but by an academic education well above average for the times.[16]

The social origins and ascent of the western mining magnate support the traditional view of the big businessman of the Gilded Age as being a self-made man. Although the mining frontier, like the rest of the nation, practiced racial and ethnic discrimination, it was evidently more democratic than the older, more settled areas of the country in extending opportunities for outstanding industrial success. In short, the western mining frontier was no more tolerant than eastern society, but it apparently was more open. While offering no final proof, the data in this study corroborate Turner's claim that the frontier promoted vertical social mobility, or the freedom to rise.

Two

MOTIVATION AND MIGRATION

WHAT COMMON MOTIVES prompted aspiring bonanza kings to abandon their homes for the uncertain promise of the frontier? Having worked on their fathers' farms or as clerks in banks or general merchandising houses, future magnates evidently sought to escape the toil of the farm life or the monotony of clerical work. As a storekeeper and boarding-house proprietor on Colorado's mining frontier in the 1860s and 1870s, the wife of Horace Tabor, the multimillionaire silver king, reported, "I never saw a country settled up with such greenhorns as Colorado. They were mostly from farms and some clerks."[1]

Other men were driven west by economic dislocation. Hard times encouraged the discontented to join the California gold rush. John P. Jones, destined to become one of the fifty or more Comstock millionaires, was typical of this group:

> Times were bad just before the discovery of gold in California. It was the era following the Mexican War, prices were down to the lowest ebb, and there was little available money in the country. The bottom almost dropped out of everything, and many of the young men decided to seek new fields of endeavor in some other part of our country. I was twenty years of age at the time, living with father's family in Cleveland, which at that time was a village of only one thousand people. I contracted the "California fever," as it was called . . . and . . . reached California in September, 1849. I immediately scampered for the gold fields.[2]

At least two bonanza kings, Almarin B. Paul and Samuel T. Hauser, sought to escape illness or family problems. Paul fled from Saint Louis in 1849: "As the death rate from cholera was still about two hundred a day, I began to have a desire to get away."[3] The West was for health seekers as well as for wealth seekers. Living well into his eighties as a prosperous mining investor and inventor in California, Paul evidently found his expectations fulfilled on the frontier. Hauser came to the Montana gold camps of Alder Gulch and Bannack in 1862 in part to avoid family problems caused by the Civil War. His pro-Southern sympathies conflicted with his father's allegiance to the Union.[4] Soon Hauser was profitably interested in various frontier enterprises including banking, mining, and land reclamation.

The experiences of Jones, Paul, and Hauser suggest that it took more than simply the discovery of gold to start a gold rush. In fact, the existence of gold in Georgia, California, Colorado, South Dakota, and Alaska was known long before the initial rushes to these areas. It appears that all five of these rushes took place during periods of unusual national excitement or upheaval which seemed to motivate men to seek adventure.[5]

Just as there were forces driving men from their homes, so there were forces attracting them to the mining frontier. Some came to the West, as they still do today, because it offered an appropriate natural setting for leisure and recreation. Jerome B. Wheeler, a successful New York merchant, vacationed in the Rockies near Aspen, Colorado, in 1883. His temporary residence, however, soon became permanent when he discovered that Colorado contained attractions more rewarding than her scenic mountains. Wheeler turned Aspen into a leading silver-mining center before twentieth-century skiers rediscovered its recreational value.[6]

Other bonanza kings attributed their migration to a love of nature and the freedom of movement provided by the wilderness. Dennis Sheedy, the smelting king, echoed this view of the frontier, "I think, perhaps, it was this love of the great outdoors instilled into me in my youth [in New England] that first impelled me to venture into the West and to make the open world my home for many years."[7]

In a letter to his brother Edward, Henry R. Wolcott, a Colorado smelting entrepreneur, gave this glowing report of life in Central City in 1870, reflecting the various attractions which contributed to western settlement: "I should like to see you, Ed, and out here, too. There are some splendid fellows here; plenty of good tobacco, good parties of the stag variety; good stories, good board, light air, lots of reading matter, lots of wood and oil; good shave (hot-water arrangement); good bed blankets, (no sheets); and I have a devilish smart 'dorg.' "[8] Edward must have been impressed with this list of Central City's merits as he soon joined his brother and became a leading mining lawyer and politician in Colorado.

Of all the motives and arguments for coming to the mining frontier, the quest for wealth was the most compelling. The new El Dorado promised ambitious entrepreneurs a chance to make their fortune. As a farmer and miner in Missouri during the 1840s, George Hearst caught the gold fever:

> I recollect talking over California with my mother. She did not like it at all, but when I told her they were making forty and fifty dollars a day there and that it seemed to me it was by far the best thing to do, as it was pretty hard pulling where we were, she said that if they were doing that well she had no doubts I would make something too, and she agreed for me to go.[9]

Mrs. Hearst underestimated her son's chances. He became one of the most successful silver and gold miners of the late nineteenth century.

Nathaniel P. Hill also found the promise of instant wealth irresistible. In 1857, he wrote a friend that he regarded the West as "the most favored portion of our country" and that one day he might "emigrate to one of those flourishing cities to seek [his] fortune."[10] Seven years later the occasion arose. While a professor of chemistry at Brown University, he was employed by a group of New England manufacturers to investigate the mineral potential of a one-million-acre tract in southern Colorado. Optimistic about his new position, Hill wrote his wife from Denver: "This presents one of the finest opportunities to make not only some money, but also some fame that has ever presented itself to me. If it turns out that the tract is rich in precious metals, I want no better fortune."[11] By the 1870s, fortune had indeed come to Hill as the prominent manager of one of Colorado's leading smelting plants, the Boston and Colorado.

Hill learned that such wealth was not easily attained. Much of Colorado's gold and silver ore had to undergo a costly, exacting smelting process before producing marketable bullion. Jerome B. Chaffee, who had come to Colorado in 1860 to make a big strike, had to learn a similar lesson. Discouraged by his initial efforts, he found reason to express the contradiction, doubtless felt by many, between the high expectations and harsh realities of life on the mining frontier: "The truth is, this getting rich quick out here is mighty doubtful; there are ten chances of getting killed or dying of disease to one of living and getting rich."[12] Despite his misgivings, Chaffee persevered to find success on the Bobtail gold lode (a large body or vein of ore) in Gilpin County. Profitable investments in such other Colorado districts as silver-rich Leadville made him one of the bonanza kings.

Perhaps the timing of the western migration of these ambitious entrepreneurs gives the most convincing evidence of their economic motivation. The majority of the aspiring miners in this study joined the westward movement at an early stage, usually during the initial rush to the various mining regions when prospects for the big strike were most encouraging. The California gold rush of 1849–50 attracted approximately one-third of the future mining magnates, If one considers the period 1851–54 as well, California introduced two-fifths of these hopefuls to the mining frontier. In 1859, the Pike's Peak rush initiated mining in Colorado. By 1865, one-fifth of the fifty moguls had received their introduction to mining in the territory. The rushes to Nevada, Montana, and Idaho during the early 1860s attracted other bonanza kings. With the exception of Hauser and Enos Wall, later the owner of extensive copper properties in Utah's Bingham Canyon, the initial placer-mining booms brought few of the fifty magnates to Montana or Idaho.[13] However, many "Old Californians," such as Paul and Hearst, crossed the Sierra Nevada when the discovery of Nevada's Comstock Lode foreshadowed the exploitation of silver on a scale hitherto unknown in the United States.

Migration to the mines was sometimes as eventful as life in the diggings. California argonauts traveled overland by wagon along the Oregon Trail, by steamer via the Isthmus of Panama, or by sailing ship around Cape Horn. The three routes were almost equally demanding. Jones came to the coast by way of Cape Horn in the 160-ton lake schooner *Eureka*. According to him, although the voyage "was a long, hard trip it was filled with interest for us all."[14] Darius O. Mills chose the Panama route, usually the quickest but most expensive way to the mines. However, once across the Isthmus, he was unable to secure passage to San Francisco. The crews of previous northbound vessels had deserted for the mines, leaving their ships moored in the San Francisco harbor. Mills turned to the west coast of South America, and at the Peruvian seaport of Callao chartered a bark. Arriving in San Francisco in June 1849 over six months after leaving New York, he established a merchandising business which led to banking and mining investments, notably on the Comstock.[15]

Rich strikes during the 1860s in Colorado, Nevada, Idaho, and Montana and during the 1870s in Utah and South Dakota caused migration routes to develop in an eastward as well as a westward direction. Following his California and Nevada experiences, Hearst ranged as far afield as Utah in 1872 and South Dakota in 1877 soon after major strikes opened these areas. Such other "Old Californians" as James Fair and John Mackay tried their luck in Idaho, losing several thousand dollars in an unproductive mine and mill in 1867. The Comstock later bestowed a much kinder fate on these two men. The mining fields of the Northwest attracted migrants simultaneously from the Midwest, East, and Far West. Having been a miner in California, Nevada, and Utah, Marcus Daly came to Montana in the mid-1870s. His future adversary in the struggle for control of the Montana copper industry, William Andrews Clark, was already there, having arrived in 1863 by way of Iowa and Colorado. Unlike Idaho and Montana, Colorado was populated largely by westward-moving settlers.[16] Such major mining entrepreneurs as Chaffee and David Moffat abandoned their positions with a midwestern real estate company and a bank, respectively, for the mineral wealth of the Colorado Rockies.

Alleged or real advantages notwithstanding, prospective bonanza kings, like most prospectors, regarded the West as only a temporary residence. They hoped to make a lucky strike or quick business profit before returning home. Moffat, for example, came to Denver in 1860 with the intention of building a $75,000 fortune on which to live in the East.[17] Some men, such as Thomas Selby, the California smelting and refining pioneer, and Tabor, came west to pay off debts incurred in the East or Midwest. Both intended originally to stay only until their debts were cleared. Tabor gave this account of his migration to Colorado in 1859:

> I came out here for the purpose of mining, because we [he and his wife] knew nothing of this country except as a mining country. I had to borrow money to enter my land down there at Kansas; I had to mortgage it and I came for the express purpose of trying to make money enough out here to redeem that land. . . . At that time I really had no other idea, except to redeem that land. . . . After I got here I liked the country well enough to stay.[18]

Preoccupation with quick wealth left little time or inclination to build a permanent, stable material and spiritual life on the frontier. Only when such entrepreneurs as Tabor recognized that successful industrial mining was a slow, often unpredictable process did their attitudes about the West become more realistic. Those who overcame their initial disillusionment either eventually decided to stay or were forced to remain for financial reasons.

Whether approached from the East or the Far West, by wagon or ship, the mining frontier promised many different opportunities for aspiring bonanza kings. It offered some an escape from the boredom, disease, or economic hardship of their former homes. Others were attracted by the freedom and adventure of living close to nature. However, the subjects of this study regarded the opportunity for economic self-improvement as the most compelling motive for migration.

Profit-minded mining entrepreneurs arrived early, hoping to find the bonanza that had eluded them in other regions and in other occupations. For one of these magnates, Irving Howbert of Colorado, early disadvantage in life was almost a prerequisite for success on the frontier: "In this Western country there are singularly few men who have accomplished great success for themselves, who have been swathed during the formative period of their lives in the enervating folds of luxury."[19]

Relatively few bonanza kings could claim such an up-
bringing. In fact, according to the popular ideology of the
late nineteenth century, poor boys stood a better chance
of achieving and sustaining success than those from
wealthy families since they were supposed to have greater reason to appreciate and cultivate the values of thrift,
hard work, honesty, and sobriety. In Horatio Alger
fashion potential mining leaders could benefit from early
poverty. However, the way to wealth demanded more
than the good character allegedly fostered by lower-class
origins and the good luck traditionally associated with
Alger's heroes in his numerous nineteenth-century nov-
els.

Three

LEARNING THE TRADE

MINING LEADERS took the first step toward success only after acquiring property, labor, and capital. The acquisition of these factors of production could prove difficult in any industry, but attracting capital posed special problems in the mining industry and on the frontier. It seemed as though everyone had a promising claim or mine for sale, especially during the flush times after a significant strike. The labor force was continually replenished by unsuccessful prospectors and the immigration of skilled or semiskilled workers such as the experienced Cornish miners. The periodic collapse of such mines as those on the Comstock in the 1880s also released trained laborers for employment. Investment capital was much more scarce on the remote, economically undeveloped, and unstable mining frontier, where the expectation of great profit could quickly be dashed. Therefore, an abundant or more than adequate supply of mining properties and laborers competed for a limited amount of available capital. A student of this phenomenon has remarked that "capital for purchasing and developing mining claims always constituted the short factor of production and the point at which promotional competition remained hottest."[1]

Related to the standard factors of production and equally important to successful entrepreneurship was knowledge of mining technology. It enabled an entrepreneur to select the most promising claims and to direct his employees and capital to the best advantage when deal-

ing with the problems of deep-level mining or the smelting of refractory ores, which have a complex chemical
and metallic structure that discourages easy separation.
Presumably, individuals who could acquire the necessary factors of production, including technological expertise, had the best chance to succeed.

The entrepreneur's acquisition of mining properties
presented his initial challenge. Assuming that an early
arrival on the frontier facilitated selection of the most
promising claims or mines, did future magnates prospect
or invest in major mining regions or districts soon after
the discovery of important strikes? With the possible
exception of Simeon Wenban, an early participant in the
Cortes silver district of eastern Nevada in 1863, none of
the fifty bonanza kings discovered a major mining district. However, some were original locators of mining
properties they later developed into very productive
enterprises. Winfield S. Stratton located the Independence mine in Colorado's Cripple Creek district in 1891,
soon after a wandering cowboy, Bob Womack, discovered
the district. After working the mine at substantial profit
for nearly a decade, Stratton sold out to British investors
for ten million dollars. Sandy Bowers of Nevada was
another original locator who turned his property into a
fortune. Prospecting in Gold Canyon in 1859 when the
Comstock Lode was discovered, Bowers located a small
claim which he combined with an adjacent one of equal
size by marrying the owner. The union soon made
Bowers the Comstock's first millionaire. Jesse Knight of
Utah was another locator who made good. Discovery of
the Humbug mine in the Tintic district during the mid-
1880s laid the foundation for his mining fortune.[2]

The cases of Stratton, Bowers, and Knight were atypi-
cal. Though the bonanza kings usually did not arrive
early enough to become original locators, they did come
in time to acquire the more promising properties. Usual-

ly they invested within a few years after the first strikes
publicized the discovery of a new district. In 1876, the
silver-lead carbonates of Leadville were made known for
the first time. By the end of the third mining season,
Horace Tabor, David Moffat, Jerome Chaffee, and Irving
Howbert, four of Colorado's most prominent mining men,
had invested extensively in the area. Their mines, including the Little Pittsburg, Maid of Erin, and Robert E.
Lee, produced silver in quantities sufficient to emphasize
the advantages of being relatively early in the field.

Moffat was particularly adept at investing in a new
district early enough to gain the greatest reward. In the
1890s, he quickly invested in the newly discovered
Colorado districts of Cripple Creek and Creede, purchasing the Victor and Anaconda in the former and the
Amethyst and Holy Moses in the latter. Such leading
entrepreneurs as Moffat often purchased mines from
their original locators.[3]

Although some of these early fortune hunters had the
ability and luck to discover promising properties, few
were able to retain them. Usually lacking the patience,
capital, or technological expertise to develop their holdings, these men were unlikely to become bonanza kings.
On the Comstock the early prospectors usually were
poor, adventurous men who quickly sold their mines and
drifted on to new fields in search of other properties.[4] Of
the nine original locators of the Comstock Lode, only two
held their claims long enough to become wealthy.

The tendency of discoverers to sell out to the industrial
entrepreneur who could command the capital and technology necessary to transform a promising claim into a
productive mine was a recurrent phenomenon throughout the West. For example, in 1872, George Hearst and
James B. Haggin bought the Ontario mine near Park City,
Utah, for $27,000 from the original locator, Herman
Budden and his associates. Hearst then cleared title to

the mine by paying $3,000 to another claimant. From 1877 to 1891, the year of Hearst's death, the Ontario paid $12,425,000 in dividends. Such successful mines as the Ophir in Nevada, the Anaconda in Montana, and the Homestake in South Dakota became the property of Hearst and his partners, directly or indirectly, through the services of original locators.[5]

If the mining entrepreneur did not acquire his properties directly from the original locator, he often negotiated the purchase through a promoter. The professional promoter was primarily a salesman who sought to market claims provided by discoverers, receiving in payment for his services a cash commission or stock in the company organized to develop the claims. Such an individual was James F. Wardner. His association with Noah Kellogg and Philip O'Rourke, the locators of Idaho's Bunker Hill and Sullivan mine induced Samuel Hauser, the Montana silver milling and smelting pioneer, to invest in the property in the mid-1880s. When the mine was subsequently sold to Simeon G. Reed of Oregon in 1887, Wardner was retained temporarily as general manager. In this capacity he and Reed discussed the wisdom of purchasing claims adjacent to the Bunker Hill.[6] Either as a salesman or a part-time administrator, the professional promoter could be instrumental in securing mining properties for the capitalist. However, success in selecting and developing properties also depended upon knowledge of mining technology.

Many of the fifty future bonanza kings gained their first technical experience as placer miners panning gold beside streams or working sluice boxes with other miners. Sometimes placer mining proved sufficiently rewarding to encourage continued employment in the industry or provided a stake allowing the miner to enter less debilitating or less seasonal occupations. Seven of the fifty entrepreneurs profited significantly from placer mining. Alvinza Hayward parlayed early success in placer mining in Amador County, California, into an industrial-mining fortune during the 1850s. He built a stamp mill in which mineral-bearing quartz ore was crushed by descending pestles known as stamps. It made money much faster than the placers. In 1864, Dennis Sheedy, a placer miner near Virginia City, Montana, worked a claim which yielded from $300 to $500 a day and sold for $2,200 when he abandoned mining for merchandising and freighting in 1865. Later Sheedy returned to the industry as a prominent Colorado smelting and refining entrepreneur. William A. Clark's early career was another placer mining success story. From 1863 to 1864, Clark and a partner netted several thousand dollars from claims they located near Bannack, Montana. The initial stake facilitated Clark's entry into merchandising and banking. By the 1870s, he had returned to mining as an active investor.[7]

Whether rewarding or not, placer mining gave prospective magnates instruction in such rudiments of mining as the use of quicksilver as an amalgamating agent in separating gold from waste rock. Although placer mining lessons were undoubtedly of limited use when applied to the more technologically demanding industrial mining, milling, and smelting, they nonetheless introduced the entrepreneur to the instability of the profession and to the uncertainty which confronted miners searching for the elusive nugget or tracing the meandering vein.

Men who remained continuously in the industry after an initial exposure to the placers became familiar with the demands of technology in deep-level mining. Many bonanza kings served an extended practical apprenticeship to learn their trade before becoming successful. For at least two, Hearst and Almarin Paul, this apprenticeship began before their migration to the West. During the 1840s, Hearst spent seven years as a copper and lead miner in Missouri, while Paul began his mining career in the Lake Superior copper mines.[8] However, practical experience in industrial mining was usually acquired in the Far West and Rocky Mountain region and usually consisted of work as a laborer, timberman, foreman, or superintendent. Sometimes it meant employment as a stamp mill or smelter builder or operator. Many incipient mining moguls alternated working for others with prospecting on their own, hoping to discover the productive mine which eluded all but the fortunate few.

Stratton's discovery and development of the Independence mine came after seventeen years of mining for himself and others. During that period he prospected most of Colorado's major mining fields. He also worked in a gold reduction mill in Summit County, Colorado, learning the pan amalgamation process. This process subjected pulverized, gold-bearing rock from the stamp mill to a second grinding with mercury in a heated pan to release the amalgam of gold and mercury. The mercury was then driven off by distillation. The knowledge gained by practical experience was increased by Stratton's academic training during his attendance at the Colorado School of Mines and Colorado College at Colorado Springs in 1884. By studying geology and mineralogy, Stratton learned how to detect mineral-bearing rocks, treat refractory ores, and conduct assays. Instruction in the latter gave him the skill to test the value of ore with a blowpipe. His training as a working miner and as a student of technology served him well during the systematic development of the Independence and other Cripple Creek properties. The American Institute of Mechanical Engineers, the United States Department of Mines, and the Colorado Scientific Society regarded the Independence as one of the most efficiently managed mines to come under their inspection.[9]

The early career of James G. Fair further exemplifies the role of technical knowledge in contributing to success. As a boy, Fair worked in a Chicago machine shop. Having come to California in 1849, he experimented successfully with placer mining at Long Bar and Rich Bar on the Feather River, but he turned to lode or vein mining as part owner of the Utica mine and stamp mill at Angels Camp in Calaveras County during the mid-1850s. By 1860, he was on the Comstock working in the Ophir and Central mines. Soon his technical experience earned him the superintendency of the Ophir and subsequently the assistant superintendency of the Hale and Norcross. Recognizing the potential of the latter, he urged John Mackay, William O'Brien, and James Flood to invest in it. In 1869, after a struggle with the Bank of California, which held controlling interest, the mine became the property of the four partners. From 1866 to 1872, it paid $1,598,000 in dividends and produced $7,822,000 from 313,000 tons of ore.[10]

The partnership dominated the Comstock for two decades. As a member of this foursome Fair became the superintendent of many Nevada properties and used his extensive technical training and managerial experience to good advantage. He operated the firm's properties efficiently, with little extravagance or waste in a region known for the squandering of stockholders' money.[11]

Thomas Kearns of Utah is another bonanza king who used his practical experience to select and occupy a strategic property. After leading the life of an itinerant prospector and teamster in such remote areas as Arizona and South Dakota from 1879 to 1883, Kearns found steady employment with the Ontario Mining Company of Park City, Utah. For six years he worked as a shift man taking out ore. After work he either prospected on his own or returned to his lodging for six or eight hours of study, examining books on mineralogy and mining geology. In late 1888, following his friend David Keith, he quit his job with the Ontario and began with the nearby Woodside mine, securing a contract to run a 200-foot tunnel through the property. Contracting exploratory or developmental work was a common practice in the mining industry, and Kearns made good use of the opportunity. During construction of the tunnel he noticed the direction of the principal vein of ore. Utilizing his knowledge of geology and mineralogy, he perceived that the vein led into the adjacent, undeveloped Mayflower mine. In partnersip with David Keith, John Judge, Albion B. Emery, and Windsor V. Rice, Kearns secured a lease on the Mayflower. Soon after beginning work in February 1889, the new owners found a rich strike, containing one hundred ounces of silver and 30 percent lead to the ton. From the vantage point of the Mayflower's underground workings, Kearns learned that the main vein ran into the Silver King mine. By 1892, Kearns and his partners were also in control of this mine, destined to become one of Utah's most famous producers of silver and lead.[12]

Like Kearns and other aspiring entrepreneurs, Thomas Walsh benefited from practical experience and self-instruction in industrial mining and geology. After receiving only a limited formal education, Walsh became a systematic prospector and self-taught student of mining technology in Colorado, preparing for the big strike that awaited him in the 1890s. As an old man looking back on a very prosperous career, he gave a newspaper reporter this account of his early training: "Shortly after I came to Colorado, I began to study geology, mineralogy, and metallurgy from a practical standpoint. I soon found that I had a natural ability—an intuitive perception, you might call it—as to the values of the ore in rock."[13]

For those not similarly gifted, formal education provided an alternate means of acquiring technical knowledge. Some magnates, either before or after taking their first regular job, received training which could complement the practical experience gained as working miners. As a miner in Missouri, Hearst briefly attended the Franklin County Mining School. As a boy in Germany, Adolph Sutro excelled in the practical curriculum of science and mathematics offered by the polytechnic schools. He must have been impressed by the efficiency and economy derived from the proper application of technology. He built a quartz-reducing mill at East Dayton, Nevada, in the early 1860s, which worked over the tailings of other mills by a new amalgamation process. Profits from this enterprise doubtless encouraged him to construct the famous Sutro Tunnel, designed to increase the efficiency of mining operations on the Comstock by facilitating the drainage of water and the removal of ore. Bela S. Buell was another mining entrepreneur who made use of his education. In 1855, at the age of nineteen, Buell graduated with a Bachelor of Science degree from Norwich University, Vermont, having completed courses in mathematics, geology, mineralogy, and civil engineering. Although he faced the problem of reducing Colorado's refractory gold ores, his mine and mill in Gilpin County were successful enough to warrant the national circulation of a detailed description by the United States mining commissioner, Rossiter W. Raymond.[14]

Such other magnates as Stratton, Clark, Joseph R. DeLamar, and Sheedy returned to school later in life to learn the mining and smelting business. Sheedy entered the smelting business in 1887, when the bank of which he was vice-president acquired the Holden Smelting Works of Denver. Unfamiliar with the methods and problems of smelting, he set out to learn:

> Up to this time I knew nothing of smelting or ores, and my only knowledge of mining was that brief period working and owning placer mines in Montana. I realized that to accomplish anything I

must master the details of the industry, and there followed three
years of incessant study, part of the time under a tutor. I read
every book upon the subject obtainable, gaining a technical as well
as a practical knowledge of the business. Night after night I
studied with the tutor, all my efforts in the day being bent to
saving money in operation and in saving the values from the ores
smelted.[15]

As president and general manager of the Holden enterprise, reorganized as the Globe Smelting and Refining
Company in 1889, Sheedy was responsible for enlarging
the plant and increasing annual production from
$200,000 in 1889 to $16,000,000 by 1907. This change
can be partially attributed to the application of the
following technological improvements:

The additions included a refinery, and parting plant to part the
gold and silver after we took it out of the lead which was done by
electricity and nitric acid, and other improvements that enabled us
to handle the product of the mine from the ore to the finished
product, or bullion. I also built a bag house of 4,800 bags, and an
improved slag furnace after designs of my own, that . . . enabled us
to obtain more values from the ore, and also to save values that
prior to this time had escaped in fumes, or in slag.[16]

Just as some bonanza kings received a basic technical
education as young men or thorough specialized training
in later life, so others were prepared for success by extensive, highly professional studies at the collegiate and
post-graduate level. Among these was John Hays Hammond, perhaps the best-known American mining engineer, with the exception of Herbert Hoover. Having
graduated from the Sheffield School of Mining at Yale
University in 1876, Hammond continued his education
at the Royal School of Mines in Freiberg, Saxony, from
1876 to 1879, because "there were no good mining
schools in the United States."[17] The thorough training
acquired at the best mining school in the world initiated
a successful career as consulting engineer, manager, and

owner of mining properties in the United States, Mexico, South America, and South Africa. In his autobiography, Hammond explained how academic training could help make one a successful practical engineer:

> I soon realized the immense advantage of technical training as I observed that a trained engineer could in a short time qualify as "practical" in the operation of mines.
>
> It did not take the educated engineer long to become more proficient in the handling of pumps and other mining machinery, in timbering the mines, in the use of explosives, and in the extraction of ore bodies, than the practical miner himself. And, of course, in the metallurgical treatment of ores he was immeasurably superior by reason of his technical knowledge.[18]

It is not surprising that many processors of ore owed their success in part to a thorough preparation in chemistry or metallurgy. The result of such training is perhaps best exemplified by the career of Nathaniel P. Hill. After graduating from Brown University, Hill remained as an instructor and professor of chemistry until 1864. During several trips to Colorado Territory, from 1864 to 1866, he purchased mining properties for himself and his eastern business associates and, more important, observed the great loss of gold in stamp mills worked by the amalgamation process. As the surface-oxidized ore was replaced by sulphide refractory ore, the loss increased. The problem faced Buell and other early mill operators and threatened to depress permanently Colorado's mining industry. As a trained chemist and geologist, Hill believed that much of the loss could be averted by smelting the ore into an impure mixture of sulphides called matte which could be refined or further purified in New York or Wales. He went to Swansea, Wales, a leading mineral-reduction center, for further study and returned to Colorado in 1867 to construct a smelter at Blackhawk in Gilpin County under the direction of the Boston and Colorado Smelting Company. In partnership with Richard Pearce, a famous European metallurgist, he built additional smelters at Alma and other Colorado camps and moved the main plant to Argo, near Denver, in 1878. In 1880, Hill's company was operating forty furnaces, processing 35,000 tons of ore, employing 170 men, and producing $3,907,000 in gold, silver, and copper. It has been said that Hill inaugurated the great mining era of the Rockies by recognizing that the nonoxidized, deep-level ores of the region required smelting rather than the amalgamation process.[19]

Thus, the acquisition of technical knowledge took various forms. Many bonanza kings were introduced to it on the lowest level as placer miners. However, success in industrial mining, milling, or smelting demanded more technical knowledge and experience than placer mining could provide. Therefore, nearly thirty of the fifty magnates served relatively extensive apprenticeships as lode mining prospectors, laborers, foremen, superintendents, or engineers, or, less frequently, as mill or smelter operators. In most cases, practical, on-the-job training was supplemented by independent study or by formal scientific education. The latter was especially of service to later owners of mills, smelters, or refineries.

Technical training facilitated the selection and systematic development of promising mining properties and acquainted employers with the problems of their workers, especially as they battled the elements in the underground mines of the Comstock. But capital was also needed to purchase properties, machinery, and supplies, pay employees, and finance the reduction of ore. Not only did these large-scale operations demand large amounts of capital, but they also involved high risks extending capital to an unstable and technologically experimental frontier industry. Lloyd Tevis, a prominent California financier, described the problem to a convention of American bankers in 1881:

In the loaning of money the risks were so great that even at 5, and sometimes 10 per cent per month, accumulations were comparatively small. The choice of securities was limited and the value of property uncertain. Sweeping floods, and desolating fires, due to the temporary character of building, sudden changes of population owing to the working out of old placers or the discovery of fresh ones, and fluctuations in stocks of goods drawn from distant markets, with which communication could only be had at intervals, gave even to the ordinary branches of trade a speculative character, and introduced a large element of risk into all calculations.[20]

Self-taught or academically trained miners like Daly, Mackay, Hammond, or Grant had sufficient technological knowledge but insufficient capital. On many occasions they had to acquire funds from mining financiers like Tevis, Haggin, or Darius O. Mills. Such men might have had some practical mining experience, but primarily they had pursued other occupations before investing heavily in the industry.

An examination of these frontier occupations reveals those jobs, aside from mining itself, which promoted success in the industry. The fields listed in table 7 were

TABLE 7
DOMINANT PRIOR OCCUPATIONS OF
WESTERN MINING LEADERS

Occupation	Numerical Frequency
Merchandising	17
Banking	13
Freighting	5
Public Officeholding	5
Law	2
Carpentry	2
Cattle Raising	1
Education	1
Total Cases (= 37)	46

pursued immediately before successful and extensive participation in mining. Where it was difficult to determine the dominant prior occupation of individuals who simultaneously held two or more jobs, several were listed. Combinations such as merchandising and banking, or freighting and merchandising frequently appear. Listing of multiple occupations accounts for the discrepancy between the total number of cases and the total number of occupations. Men who were almost exclusively miners before finding success in the industry are not listed.

Why did merchants and bankers often become successful mining entrepreneurs? The well-stocked merchant was likely to make large, quick profits from the boom following a significant strike, when miners were both eager and able to pay for his goods. In periods of high demand, inflated prices often produced the investment capital necessary for success in large-scale mining. Isaac Rogers, a merchant in Virginia City, Montana, during the mid-1860s, reported that profits from the sale of most commodities ran as high as 25 percent.[21]

Much greater profits were made by Paul, whose career aptly illustrates the tactics and advantages of frontier merchandising. Before joining the California gold rush, Paul purchased $10,000 worth of hardware goods for a mercantile business he and a doctor friend from Saint Louis intended to establish in the new El Dorado. Arriving in 1849, Paul and his partner were soon situated in a store in the makeshift city of Sacramento. Of his first year in business, Paul reported: "Our stock was mainly building hardware, but we soon added a grocery department. Business was so heavy that we decided to take in . . . a partner. . . . All through the summer [1850] we did a big business, sales running at times to over three thousand dollars a day, while the profits were very large.[22] Locks, spring balances, and tacks were particularly marketable. From a $50 investment in the latter, Paul realized over $1,700. Having purchased spring balances for $4 per dozen, he sold sixteen dozen for $3,200 to a competitor seeking to corner the market. Even trivial items like tea bells were in heavy demand:

> I had a lot of small tea bells that cost two dollars a dozen. These I sold for half an ounce of gold each at first [$8–$9], but, being reprimanded by my next door neighbor, who had some of the same, for selling so cheap, I put them up to an ounce and sold the remainder easily at that price. The gamblers used these bells to call for drinks when the game began to lag.[23]

Capitalizing on good timing and the high demand for basic commodities in a rapidly populated, underdeveloped area, a merchant like Paul could acquire sufficient investment capital. In the fall of 1850, with inventory low after the prosperous summer and with Sacramento floods threatening his business, Paul sold out and turned to mining. His initial California venture, the Yuba River Gold Dredging Company, showed little profit. In 1851, with Hearst, he built one of the first stamp mills in Nevada County, California. Although additional capital and technological experimentation were needed to perfect methods for saving the gold, the enterprise was sufficiently promising to sustain his interest in the industry. Before removing to the Comstock in 1860, he had become one of Nevada County's most prominent stamp mill operators.[24]

The grubstake system was frequently the vehicle by which merchants invested in mining. Perhaps Tabor best illustrates how the grubstake system could make a merchant into a bonanza king. In July 1877, Tabor and his wife opened a grocery and general store in Leadville, Colorado. In the same year, Tabor supplied two prospectors, August Rische and George F. Hook, with seventeen dollars for room and board in exchange for a one-third interest in whatever they discovered. As a relatively successful merchant in other Colorado camps, Tabor had grubstaked needy miners before with little return on his investment. This time proved different. As the two miners reached hard rock, he supplied them with hand drills, a sledge, and blasting powder. His total outlay of sixty-four dollars was richly repaid in 1878 when they discovered the body of silver ore which became the famous Little Pittsburg mine. After exploiting the mine for two years at considerable profit, Tabor sold his interest for one million dollars to Chaffee and Moffat.[25]

Frontier merchants like Tabor often were news reporters, general advisers, and letter writers and readers for their customers. Therefore, they could sometimes avail themselves of inside information when making mining investments. Unlike such superintendents as Fair or Kearns, who learned the secrets of the trade from underground veins in remote drifts or shafts, merchants were more apt to be instructed by talkative patrons. While they were owners of the Auction Lunch Saloon in San Francisco, Flood and O'Brien, who later became members of the Comstock's "Bonanza Firm," received their education from mining men and stock dealers. From these customers the partners obtained advantageous mining information, enabling them to become prosperous stockbrokers. Investments in several northern California mines convinced them to sell their saloon in 1866 and concentrate on mining. Outstanding success came in the early 1870s, when, in association with Fair and Mackay, they helped engineer the purchase of the Consolidated Virginia and California mines on the Comstock.[26]

In addition to his other functions, the frontier merchant often served as a banker. If he was the owner of a safe in a well-protected building, the merchant could easily enter banking. Mrs. Tabor said of the store she and her husband owned in California Gulch, Colorado, "We had a good deal of money to take care of, we had the only safe in the country and had to keep everybody's treasures in that safe."[27]

As a banker, the local storekeeper could also become a speculator in gold. Merchant-bankers such as Tabor, Moffat, Clark, and Mills often bought gold dust from prospectors. During the 1860s, Colorado miners received $12 to $16 per ounce, depending upon the amount of foreign matter in their ore.[28] Frontier bankers either sold the dust to national mints or shipped it to eastern bankers in exchange for coin or paper currency. According to a former president of Wells, Fargo and Company, "the profits on the business were good—there was a margin on the gold and the rate of exchange was high."[29] During the early 1870s, Clark's Montana banking firm averaged annual profits of $150,000 from the sale of gold dust and bullion.[30]

By enlisting the services of such eastern banks as the American Exchange Bank of New York, frontier bankers were able to raise sufficient liquid capital to invest in the mining industry. The money was acquired by selling gold dust through these correspondent banks either for drafts or security upon which loans could be drawn at a lower rate of interest than was available on the frontier. Hauser, who in 1880 controlled all three national banks in Montana, acquired liquid capital in this manner:

> Upon sale, gold coin was reserved and this was often converted into currency or deposited in the correspondent bank. For its services the correspondent bank charged one, and sometimes two, commissions. The balances thus accruing in the correspondent bank were used partly to purchase paper currency needed in Helena, but chiefly left on deposit to cover drafts which had been sold in Helena against the bank.[31]

Buying and selling ore gave western bankers not only

investment capital but also knowledge of the most promising districts and mines in which to invest. Ore-pur-
chasing agents employed by Hauser's Helena bank often
recommended favorable prospects. If Hauser was interested, he could invest while the cost of claims was still
nominal. This knowledge of where to invest, in part,
explains his entry into Montana's Butte mining district,
where he established a branch bank in 1877.[32]

Usually western bankers became mining entrepreneurs when loans advanced to miners could not be
repaid. In 1875, Bill Farlin located the Travona mine,
the first significant quartz silver property in the Butte
district. To process the ore he built the Dexter mill.
However, without sufficient capital to develop his properties, he was forced to borrow thirty thousand dollars
from the Deer Lodge Bank partially owned by Clark.
Unable to meet the payments on his loan, Farlin turned
over his holdings as security to Clark, who was to
manage them until the loan could be repaid. When the
property fortuitously failed to return a profit, the bank
foreclosed. Clark ultimately became the sole owner of the
mill and mine, which began to produce rich ore. Many
other claims came under his control as unliquidated
collateral for bank loans and became the basis for his
sizable silver and copper fortune of the 1880s and
1890s.[33]

As creditors of mining concerns, bankers were strategically placed to become mine and mill owners when
depression hit the industry. During the first six years of
development, the Comstock Lode produced ore worth
over fifty million dollars. In 1865, many of the bonanzas
were exhausted at about the 500-foot level. During the
ensuing depression, most banks were reluctant to extend
credit to the industry at reduced rates. An exception, the
Bank of California, organized in 1864 by William C.
Ralston and Mills, advanced loans to languishing mill

and mine companies at a monthly rate of 2 percent interest, less than half the conventional rate. By this tactic, William Sharon, the director of the bank's Virginia City branch, eliminated competing banks. As mines fell deeper into borrasca, or barren rock, and mills stopped work for want of ore, owners were forced to default on their loans. The inevitable result was foreclosure by the bank. The first mill acquired was the Swansea Mill of Lyon County, in May 1866. Within a year, seven others had been acquired. To purchase and manage the mills, the bank in 1867, established the Union Mill and Mining Company, which included Mills, Ralston, and Sharon among its charter members. To secure ore for their mills, these bankers gave credit only to mines willing to send ore to the Union Mill and Mining Company.[34]

The bank also secured direct control of mines. When advancing capital to struggling miners, the bank took stock certificates as security. These certificates conferred voting rights on their holders, enabling bank members to select the directors of mining companies. By this means the bank officials could feed their mills and starve the competition. When the discovery of new ore bodies in the early 1870s revived production on the Comstock, the Bank of California was in a position to reap the harvest.[35]

The individual careers of the bonanza kings reveal the immediate problems they had to overcome to achieve success. By virtue of practical mining experience, independent study, and formal scientific education, many mining moguls obtained the technological expertise required by the industry. At times, trained or experienced miners like Paul or Clark pursued such occupations as merchandising or banking which produced investment capital. Jobs as mine superintendents, merchants, or bankers also offered means for the profitable application of capital or technology. Privileged information, grub-stakes, and loans became avenues to success in the hands of enterprising miners and speculators sensitive to the advantages of good investment timing. The investor could select wisely and develop efficiently promising properties if he possessed capital and technical knowledge. The value of both is clearly expressed by the requirements of mining the Homestake. Since unusually large quantities of ore would have to be processed en masse, the Homestake would require capital on an extensive scale and a high degree of technical and organizational ability. Such skill was as inaccessible to the prospector as was large-scale capital. To be run successfully, the Homestake had to be operated as a big business.[36]

Big business meant that property, labor, capital, and technology not only had to be acquired by the entrepreneur but also managed and coordinated effectively so that he could achieve and sustain success. The apprenticeship afforded by education and by previous mining and nonmining occupations introduced him to the requirements of the task ahead. He was learning the trade.

FOUR

PROPERTY: STRATEGY FOR SUCCESS

THE ENTREPRENEUR who sought to acquire and manage mining properties profitably soon realized that natural limitations were placed on his efforts. Mining was an extractive industry and was inherently unstable. The supply of mineral resources was limited, irreplaceable, and varied in richness. Indeed, the typical nineteenth-century mining community had a life cycle of boom to bust. Following a brief period of flush production, the mining camp might be rescued temporarily from the ensuing depression by new discoveries, greater capital investment, technological improvements, or more scientific knowledge, or the former boom area might struggle on for a number of years with a dwindling annual output and an ever shrinking labor force. In any case, the ghost town was the inevitable fate of most mining communities.[1]

The natural instability of the industry was intensified by contested ownership. Title to properties was difficult to clear and necessitated an appeal to imperfect local and federal mining laws which sometimes created more problems than they solved. According to Hubert H. Bancroft, "of all the avocations out of which men have wrested fortunes, mining may be accounted the most problematical. There are in it so many of the elements of chance that even industry, skill, and perseverance are frequently balked of their proper results."[2] The entrepreneurs who became successful took advantage of the industry's economic fluctuations by carefully purchasing, consolidating, and selling claims and mines when the market was

most receptive. The problem of legal insecurity was overcome by the consolidation of properties and by political
tactics designed to secure an uncontested title. Industrial success, in part, depended upon the entrepreneur's
ability to acquire, consolidate, and dispose of his property in a timely and systematic fashion.

Successful entrepreneurs were likely to invest in districts soon after discovery, when promising claims were
available and before their value became inflated. Good
investment timing also depended upon fluctuations in
mineral production. When hard times hit a district, new
opportunities to purchase mines were created. The investor found himself operating in a buyer's market, able to
purchase depreciated property on the assumption that
the industry could be revived. Bankers invariably capitalized on this situation, but miners with sufficient funds
and technical knowledge also seized the opportunities
created by depression.

From 1864 to 1872, production on the Comstock lan-
guished. The absence of new bonanzas and the exhaustion of old ones had forced the value of mining properties
down from the heights of the preceding boom period. For
example, the Gould and Curry mine, which was selling
at $6,300 per "foot" on July 1, 1863, dropped to $4,550 on
April 1, 1864, and to $900 on July 30, 1864. Unpopular
stock assessments and loss of public confidence further
decreased the price of stock. In 1870, the Crown Point,
one of the most productive mines of the flush times, was
worth only $2 a share. In that year, superintendent John
P. Jones, who had come to the Comstock in 1867 after a
career in California mining and politics, found indications of rich ore at a low level. The prospect evidently
failed to interest the principal owners, members of the
Bank of California. Jones subsequently turned to Alvinza Hayward, an old friend from his California mining
days. After a prosperous quartz-mining career in the

Mother Lode, Hayward had profited from Comstock investments in association with the Bank of California. He had sufficient capital and faith in Jones's expertise to invest. Together they purchased nearly 5,000 of the Crown Point's 12,000 shares at an average price of about $5 a share. As the stock began to soar, Hayward bought an additional 1,000 shares for $90 to $180 each, which gave him effective control of the property. Absolute control was achieved in 1871, when he purchased 4,100 shares from William Sharon of the Bank of California for $1,400,000, or slightly over $340 per share. Buying in quantity at deflated prices had facilitated securing control of the mine and at the same time had boosted the market value of outstanding shares. However, Sharon's price was not excessive in comparison to the $1,825 a share for which the stock sold in 1872, when the Crown Point went into bonanza.[3] During the 1870s, the mine paid $10,730,000 in dividends and became one of the four most productive mines in the history of the Comstock.

While Jones and Hayward were acquiring the Crown Point, the four Irishmen, John Mackay, James Fair, James Flood, and William O'Brien, were buying up shares of the Consolidated Virginia. Organized from several early claims by the "bank crowd" in 1867, this mine had never produced a bonanza. Its shares sold for $1 in 1870 and $2 in 1871. Having been successful a few years before with the Hale and Norcross, whose stock also had been greatly depreciated at the time of purchase, the four partners regarded the Consolidated Virginia as a good speculative investment. They acquired the mine in 1871 for approximately $80,000 and began exploring at depths of 500 feet and 1,167 feet. By 1874, new shafts and costly new machinery to overcome the intense heat and excess water of deep-level mining had indicated the discovery of an unprecedented ore body. Early in 1875, shares sold for $700. According to Dan De

Quille, a leading Comstock journalist, in 1876 the mine
was extracting 500 tons of ore per day, yielding a daily
average of $50,000.[4] Production on this scale under-
scored the remarks of a contemporary observer that "Mr.
Fair, as well as Mr. Mackay . . . knows . . . when the
market is in bonanza and borrasca . . . when to go in or
go out."[5]

In 1896, Thomas Walsh's discovery and development
of the gold-rich Camp Bird mine near Ouray, Colorado,
reflected a similar understanding. Ouray had been a
productive silver-mining district in the 1870s and the
early 1880s. By the 1890s, a decline in the price and
production of silver had made owners eager to sell their
claims, unmindful that another, more precious metal
awaited further exploration. According to his daughter,
Walsh was not apt to follow the example of "the careless
prospectors who ceased to be . . . methodical in their
search; who were always ready to assume that the first
prospectors to look at any piece of ground had been
thorough."[6] He bought some claims, including an old
silver-lead mine dump. "Out of the dump Father found
tons of 'waste' that when assayed showed values of
$3,000 a ton. Indeed, it was from the dump of . . . [an]
abandoned mine that he got some of the first of the
extraordinary riches of the Camp Bird."[7]

Some mining entrepreneurs helped depress the market in order to capitalize on potentially productive
claims. When Marcus Daly acquired an interest in the
Anaconda silver mine in 1881, Butte was still a silver-
mining center. In fact, district production did not climax
until 1887, when 400 tons of ore were treated daily by
five mills with a total of 290 stamps. In the meantime,
some mine owners feared that the appearance of copper
signaled the approaching exhaustion of the valuable
silver ore. Daly was not concerned. He believed that the
Anaconda would be much more valuable as a copper

producer than it had been as a silver mine. He closed the mine and asked his associates, James Haggin, Lloyd Tevis, and George Hearst, for developmental capital. The value of adjacent properties declined in response to the Anaconda's closing, enabling Daly and his partners to buy up these mines at reasonable prices. By the 1890s, the development of electric power and light had created a demand for copper which made Butte one of the world's leading copper centers.[8]

Thus, the boom-to-bust cycle of mining allowed shrewd investors to profit from the lack of expertise or capital of others. They were careful to minimize the risks of purchasing such unproven properties as undeveloped claims and underdeveloped mines. Some investors followed the tactics of cautious gamblers. Darius O. Mills, who had a reputation as a conservative Sacramento banker when he helped organize the Bank of California in 1864, was such a man. He agreed only reluctantly to Sharon's plan to extend bank funds to the owners of depressed Comstock mills and mines in the 1860s, an investment which was later repaid many times over. According to a contemporary observer, Mills was a careful, methodical businessman with "just enough gambling instinct to look for sure things before he gambled."[9] As a former editor of the Virginia City *Territorial Enterprise* remarked, "With him business was an exact science, around which no visible evidence of chance lingered, and so as an exact businessman he was infallible."[10]

Dennis Sheedy had a similar philosophy. He would not invest in any operation until he had fully calculated all the contingencies. His thorough, patient education in mining and smelting upon purchase of the Holden Smelting Works reflects the methodical management of the good businessman and helps explain his success.[11]

In order to limit the uncertainties of purchasing unproven properties, some entrepreneurs never gave more for a mine than the value of ore in sight. Walsh and Hearst were particularly faithful to this rule.[12] Both had sufficient technical experience and training to assess the visible and estimate the hidden value of a good prospect. F. Augustus Heinze was another entrepreneur whose success could be partially attributed to caution and training. The son of a prosperous New York dry-goods merchant, Heinze was educated at the Brooklyn Polytechnic Institute and the Columbia University School of Mines. After graduating from Columbia in 1889, he went to Butte, Montana, and joined the engineering staff of the Boston and Montana Mining Company. His work enabled him to learn the vein system of Butte Hill, thereby providing the knowledge which led to the acquisition of the Rarus mine for $400,000 in 1895. Purchase of such an expensive property was not a rash move. Careful study and preparation went into Heinze's successful business decisions. He did not buy the Rarus until he was confident of a reasonable return on his investment.[13] Heinze was evidently trying to avoid the primary cause of failure in such areas as Colorado and western Nevada in the 1860s—an unwarranted expenditure of capital and machinery on mines whose value was not fully understood. The Rarus later paid him in the millions of dollars.

Thus, when purchasing mining properties, the successful entrepreneur had to be daring enough to gamble, yet careful and shrewd enough to bet on a sure thing. Fluctuations in the output of mining districts and previous technical experience gave him the opportunity to do both. He who ultimately became richest had the staying power to survive periods of adversity and the intelligence to realize that hard times offered a unique opportunity to buy up depreciated but promising property.[14]

Success also depended upon the consolidation of claims and mines. Veins often pinched out or widened without the miner's knowledge. Mining was not an exact science, but the shrewd entrepreneur tried to make it an exact business. Once a vein or ore body was located, he purchased claims or mines adjacent to his own property, enabling him to exploit effectively a body of ore if it proved more extensive or richer outside the boundaries of the original claim.

The value of consolidation is perhaps best exemplified by those who were not always able to implement it. After Jones discovered a bonanza in the Crown Point, Hayward did not purchase the adjacent Belcher mine. William Ralston and Sharon of the Bank of California took possession on the correct assumption that the Crown Point bonanza extended into the contiguous mine. According to his nephew, Jones thought that the main vein pinched out in the Belcher. However, recent scholarsip has implied that Hayward's indifference to the Belcher was part of the negotiated settlement by which he secured absolute control of the Crown Point. When he bought Sharon's shares in the latter, Hayward also sold Sharon his interest in the Belcher. This interpretation is supported by Hayward's previous California mining career. As the owner of the profitable Badger mine in Amador County during the late 1850s, he quietly bought up shares of the adjacent Eureka mine, where the pay streak was likely to run. These and other nearby properties became collectively known as the Consolidated Amador, or Hayward mine. After extensive profitable development, the mine was sold to a joint-stock company for $600,000 and placed on the San Francisco Stock Exchange.[15] It is unlikely that Hayward would have passed up the opportunity to extend and consolidate his holdings on the Comstock if this expansion could have been achieved without sacrificing complete control of the Crown Point. The power of the Bank of California evidently made it impossible.

Entrepreneurs who successfully defied the power of the bank did so before the value and extent of their discoveries were fully appreciated. When Mackay, Fair, Flood, and O'Brien learned that part of the Consolidated Virginia bonanza extended beyond the limits of their property, they organized the adjacent claims into the California Mining Company. Shares in the California mine, which sold for $37 in September 1874, had increased to $780 by early 1875 when the four Irishmen were safely in control. The ore body of the Consolidated Virginia and California became known as the "Big Bonanza" and yielded $105,168,859 from 1873 to 1882.[16]

Claim consolidation contributed to large-scale production. From 1859 to 1882, the total output of the Comstock's sixty principal mines was $292,726,310. Some of these mines were consolidations of many smaller original properties.[17] Just as consolidation made it easier to determine the natural limits of ore bodies, so it made their extraction more systematic and efficient than would otherwise have been possible. The result was increased production and profit.

During the mid-1860s, mining in Colorado, especially in Gilpin County, exposed the inefficiency of working small claims individually. The local mining laws allowed too many small claims to be located on the most widely known gold lodes, thereby minimizing the profit of any single organization and needlessly duplicating work. Shafts were opened almost side by side, and the surface was congested with the buildings, shaft houses, machinery, and waste dumps of competing neighboring companies. During the Colorado mining depression of the late 1860s, shrewd entrepreneurs bought up adjacent claims at low prices and organized them into larger,

more efficient units. Bela S. Buell, for example, consolidated mining properties on the Vasa, Kip, and Illinois
lodes near Central City. By 1873, he had produced over a
half-million dollars from his consolidated holdings.[18]

A low-grade ore body could be profitably worked only
on a massive scale. Much of the Homestake's gold ore
averaged only $3.50 a ton, thereby necessitating the
consolidation of many adjacent claims. In 1892–93, the
Homestake Mining Company purchased new mining
properties for over $400,000. Another $103,780 was
spent in 1893–94. These acquisitions increased the visible reserves of ore from an eight years' supply in 1893 to
a twenty years' supply in 1895–96. An even more expensive buying spree followed in 1899–1900. As of 1902,
the company owned 350 claims consisting of 2,624 acres.
A near monopoly on all the ore in the vicinity of Lead,
South Dakota, encouraged efficient, centralized operations and a scale of production which makes the Homestake the largest gold mine operating in the United
States.[19]

A decline in the market value of precious metals also
fostered consolidation. As long as silver was demone-
tized, it was necessary to exploit baser metals such as
lead, which was often found with silver, in order to show
a continuous profit. Consolidation enabled miners to increase their scale of operations sufficiently to profit from
nonprecious, low-grade ores.[20]

In sum, consolidation during periods of depression
minimized the cost of purchasing properties. More important, it allowed the entrepreneur to work on a large
scale and thereby increased efficiency and production.
The bonanza king could expect a consistent, long-term
return from the systematic development of his enlarged
holdings.

Consolidation was also designed to avoid litigation.
Owners of productive mines often had to contend with

blackmailers, who would purchase adjacent properties, sink shafts into the paylode, and claim it as their own. The technique was explained by Victor M. Clement, superintendent of the Bunker Hill and Sullivan mine, in a letter to his employer, Simeon G. Reed, the Portland mining investor, in 1890:

> There are two characters to the value of mining properties—one mine may have a value, owing to its real intrinsic worth; another . . . may have a value by being so situated as to harass the working of the really valuable mine—in mining camps one is looked upon as much of a legitimate enterprise as the other. This is a deplorable condition of things in the mining business, but then that is the way it is.[21]

Often an established company either had to buy these less productive, adjacent properties at exorbitant prices or face a lengthy and costly court fight. In 1901, Jerome Wheeler of Aspen, Colorado, commented on this necessity: "During the last eighteen years many suits have been instituted against me by designing and unscrupulous persons, who claimed equities in silver mines which were fairly and honestly purchased by me. During that period I have been obliged to pay large legal fees in an effort to protect my interests."[22]

Under these circumstances the precautionary purchase of adjacent claims was advisable. An original locator of the Bunker Hill and Sullivan, for example, advised Reed to purchase the property adjoining the Sullivan: "My reason for saying this is simply as follows, you prevent petty fogging shyster Lawyers from blackmailing you out of money. They have strikers in their employ that are dangerous men."[23] Upon acquisition of Utah's Silver King mine in 1892, David Keith and Thomas Kearns bought some ground from the Park Mining Company which bordered the Silver King on two sides. According to the *Park Record* of Park City, Utah, for May 28, 1892, the property was purchased to preclude any litigation that might arise "from the working of the Silver King, which is proving to be a wonderfully rich mine."[24] Anticipating litigation between his Iron Clad mine and the adjacent Bright Diamond of Ouray, Walsh attempted to buy the latter but found the owners unwilling to sell. In late 1896, he confessed to his partner, "I sought the Bright Diamond more to protect the Iron Clad from litigation than because of its value as a mine or because of the iron it carried."[25]

If an entrepreneur could not easily prove title to his primary properties or was unable to protect them by acquiring a circle of adjacent secondary holdings, he inevitably faced contested ownership. This required an appeal to mining laws. When the trans-Mississippi mining frontier was opened in 1848, miners were trespassers on the national public domain. There were no federal mining laws whereby claims might be located and protected. Therefore, it became customary for the miners themselves to draft district regulations, later upheld or standardized by western legislatures, which conferred possessory title on mining properties. However, these local regulations operated without federal authorization and were often imprecise. In White Pine, Nevada, a typical mining district, laws did not require a miner to register the exact location of his claim according to definite landmarks.[26] If one's right to work a particular claim was challenged, title was difficult to clear.

California mining law also made title to lode claims difficult to prove. Dispensing with Spanish and English precedents, which defined the underground boundaries of such claims as the downward extension of the surface boundaries, California law entitled the owner of the upper part of the vein to follow its "dips, spurs, angles, and variations" wherever they might lead, even under another's property. As the practice spread throughout the West, it became subject to much litigation.[27]

In western Nevada mining experts and the courts
could not agree on the geological definition of the Comstock Lode. Were the ore bodies separate ledges or the
spurs and angles of a parent lode? More precisely, did
they exist in the form of narrow veins, separated by
clearly defined walls of barren rock, or as deposits in one
great fissure that constituted a single lode along the foot
of Mount Davidson?[28] Since the mining laws of the Gold
Hill and Virginia districts adopted California precedents, the issue had to be settled before title could be
proved.

The issue was first raised in the lengthy litigation between the Burning Moscow Company and the Ophir
Company, of which Hearst was part owner. The Ophir
was the original mine on the Comstock; consequently its
owners supported the single-lode theory, which would
give them the right, theoretically, to engross the entire
body of ore. The Burning Moscow Company, however,
claimed a piece of ground purchased by the Ophir as a
complete ledge separate from the Ophir's holdings. The
Burning Moscow Company obviously supported the mul-
tiple-ledge theory. Disputed ownership was argued on
two fronts—in underground conflict on the contested
border of the mines and in the courtroom, where territorial judges made and reversed decisions on the geology
of the lode. The legal contest, which was waged largely
from 1860 to 1863, cost over a million dollars and caused
the market value of both mines to fluctuate. Moreover, it
initiated an intensive period of contested ownership on
the Comstock until 1866, costing over ten million dollars
and involving over 250 suits and nearly every valuable
mine.[29]

These early years on the Comstock were particularly
corrupt because mining entrepreneurs tried to discourage rival claimants and to increase their holdings. To
secure favorable decisions, mine owners were not re-

luctant to bribe the judges. A contemporary newspaper editor cynically described the process:

> The trouble was really not so much that they [the judges] were corrupt, for that was a point of which all parties were only too ready to take advantage, but that they would not stay bought—a fact that entirely demoralized the game and made it the most chance one ever known, whereas litigants felt there should be some certainty even in buying judges. There was no affected coyness or modesty on the part of the judges. They sent out their brokers and demanded a specific amount as the price of a favorable decision. There was no objection to that; it was straightforward and business-like. But the howl came when a mining company, after squarely meeting the judicial demand, encountered an adverse decision, only to learn that the opposing company had made a higher bid and won out.[30]

Another critic of Comstock courtroom practices remarked that "the courts were presided over in great part by judges who in the east had been given appointments because of political service rendered congressmen; the majority of them knew little of the science of the law and nothing at all of the complications they would meet in the west; many of them were as corrupt as they were stupid."[31] Witnesses were also for sale. Some charged more than others, but each had his price for the manufacture of suitable testimony. "No facts were so clear and well established that they could not be controverted by a troop of hired liars, and the trials became conflicts, in which witnesses were pitted against each other on the ground of numbers rather than of competence or character."[32] Jurors were also bought, though less openly and less frequently perhaps than witnesses.

When such tactics became too costly or too unreliable, entrepreneurs were forced to seek a more predictable and orderly way of settling disputed ownership. The problem was, in part, resolved by Nevada's admission to the Union in late 1864, whereby a state judiciary replaced the old territorial bench. Composed of able and trusted lawyers, the new bench rendered decisions that usually were respected. Rival claimants no longer resorted to open violence in order to settle their grievances.[33]

Just as Comstock mine owners were adjusting to a new legal environment, so the extended silence of the federal government on the subject of mineral lands abruptly ended. In the mid-1860s, Senator John Sherman of Ohio and Congressman George Washington Julian of Indiana sponsored a bill to sell the mineral lands of the public domain in order to pay off partially the Civil War debt. This challenge to the tenuous security of holding mining properties under existing local laws was met by U.S. Senator William M. Stewart of Nevada. In 1866, he succeeded in getting Congress to enact the first general mining law for lode claims, establishing a procedure for securing United States patents and sanctioning the local mining rules and customs set forth in the various district codes. The locator was entitled to follow the dip of his lode indefinitely and to exploit all its spurs and angles.[34]

The lode law was revised in 1872, when Congress specified that a claimant must locate his surface boundaries so as to include the apex, or top, of the vein. The revised law entitled him to exploit the vein as it extended downward through the sidelines but not through the endlines of his rectangular claim.[35] The California doctrine permitting unlimited access to meandering veins was thus modified. Nonetheless, the new law created a situation ripe for continued litigation. The stage was set for a reenactment of the political tactics of the early Comstock period.

The experiences of Reed with the Bunker Hill and Sullivan mine provide a case study of the consequences of the federal apex ruling. From 1889 until 1892, when he sold the mine, Reed was almost continually involved in litigation. Usually legal contests were prosecuted on a technical level. An owner could significantly enhance his chances of proving title by hiring a respected mining engineer or geologist to investigate his property. As on the Comstock, the apex principle raised difficult scientific questions requiring the special knowledge of the expert. According to John Hays Hammond, "experts in the geology of ore-bearing formations have . . . been handsomely remunerated for their investigations. After the geological findings of one of these experts was reported to the lawyers who employed him, he was retained as a witness if he could conscientiously give testimony that would further the case of his employers. There have been instances in which his conscience proved too flexible a guide."[36]

In 1889, Reed's title to the Bunker Hill and Sullivan was challenged in an apex suit by the owners of the adjacent Mammoth mine. Clement advised an examination by geologist Rossiter Raymond and mining engineer Hammond for the purpose of giving testimony to support his employer's case.[37] After Hammond's investigation, Clement corresponded with Reed:

> Hammond writes me that I better write W. S. Keyes [a noted mining engineer and metallurgist] about retaining him for our suit. In the conversation that H. had with him, he said he would want $5000 for his services. H. says that if we employ him we better do so in time as he has now several cases on hand, and besides there is the danger of the other side retaining him, should they find out that we employ experts.[38]

Clement wrote of another candidate, Professor Walter P. Jenny, who was described as "a very bright man and of great experience in these cases and not over scrupulous, having been used extensively by Geo Hearst in his suits—they all look upon him as a second Clayton [Joshua Clayton, a prominent mining engineer], except that he has no peer on the witness stand."[39]

Reed also hired Pinkerton detectives and spies disguised as miners to infiltrate the opposition. The inside

information gained in this manner could help him antici-
pate the moves of his competitors in the courtroom or in
the underground operation of the mines. Rival owners
were not above looting each other's property. In 1889,
Clement informed his boss:

> I have written to Pinkerton's Detective Agency for one of their best
> men to come immediately. . . . It will not do for us to take any more
> chances of these fellows getting the best of us by crooked work—for
> it is *absolutely* necessary for us to get the best of them in the future
> and we must employ whatever means that will gain that end.[40]

These means included providing a receptive courtroom
audience for the evidence secured and presented by technical experts, detectives, and lawyers. Judges with some
knowledge of mining were preferred. As on the Comstock, miners resented the appointment of uninformed
judges. Clement complained: "I believe we are to have
another newfledged judge—weak as a rag and knowing
nothing about mining cases as it usually happens."[41]
Judges who would not abuse the injunction ruling were
also desired. Injunction meant the loss of time, production, and profit, as the comments of Clement in 1889
testify:

> Regarding the working on the Sullivan mine, we stand *exactly* as
> we did before, the injunction is still over the mine. . . . I was fig-
> uring on our getting to work next summer and fall on the new
> plant, but the Lord knows whether that will be possible. This loss
> of time is exceedingly annoying and I am excessively tired of it; if
> there were possibilities of its continuing beyond next year, I would
> have to resign my place here, as it is for me too much loss of
> time—particularly so in matters that are extremely uncongenial. I
> see no way for myself to make any money on the outside and
> moreover would have no inclination to attempt it with the element
> in this community [Wardner, Idaho]—there are far better fields
> than this to operate in.[42]

Hoping to break the injunction, Reed applied political
pressure and secured the appointment of James H.
Beatty to the United States Circuit Court for the District

of Idaho. In 1891, he wrote Beatty: "I don't think you will have much trouble in having your Appointment confirmed, as we have now plenty of time to get in our work, and in the meantime I shall doubtless see quite a number of Senators personally, and if necessary I will visit Washington when the Senate Convenes. We would like *very much* to get a hearing on the temporary Mammouth Injunction Case."[43]

Reed also attempted unsuccessfully to elect his lawyer, William Clagett, to the United States Senate. As a senator, Clagett could theoretically have controlled the patronage necessary to place friendly judges in the Idaho courts. The following remarks by Clement reflect the sense of urgency with which this move was calculated in late 1891:

> The judiciary of our section is getting more discouraging every day, and from the situation of things I see that it becomes imperative for us to strain every muscle to place Clagett in the Senate, in order to have a sword over their heads. If Dubois [member of the opposition] gets it—having most of the Federal offices under his control, I fear very much for Northern Idaho interests—and especially for us, as most of his friends are our enemies. I am despairing of ever terminating any case that we have in the local courts, as the judge is utterly incapable of understanding complex cases. Our hope is with the Circuit Court and then, outside of Beatty, all the officers are Dubois men. We are making every effort to get into that Court all the cases we can.[44]

If the entrepreneur could not rely on the judge to decide in his favor, he was likely, as on the Comstock, to bribe jurors or witnesses. In a letter to Reed, Clement wrote: "I have not yet made terms with the . . . witnesses —I offered them $1000—for their testimony, but would not accept—I expect they will come to time after while."[45] This practice offered little assurance. Witnesses were likely to change their testimony for a higher fee. Such variables caused Clement to comment on the "depraved moral state of the country: Who is it that you can trust, but after receiving your money is ready to sell you to the next man?"[46]

Thus, whether in the Washoe district of western Nevada or in the Coeur d'Alene region of northern Idaho, corruption was an expedient, if unpredictable, means of protecting property. At a time when the public appeared to agree tacitly that the end justified the means, Clagett's remarks about the morality of Wardner, Idaho, would have aroused few objections on the mining frontier or in the nation as a whole. In this community "successful vice and corruption is looked upon as heroism."[47]

Although he used dubious political tactics, Simeon G. Reed was neither a hero nor a notable success in Idaho. He failed to realize that such tactics were designed to force the opposition to settle out of court if the suit could not be won in court. When litigation became a war of attrition, compromise was the only alternative to defeat or a pyrrhic victory. In early 1890, Clement wrote his boss about compromising with the opposition:

> I would by all means prefer to defeat them by litigation. . . . My judgment tells me however that a settlement is the better policy—for several reasons—
>
> 1st The cost to us of the litigation, even if successful would amount to us say 20 to 25 thousand dollars.
>
> 2nd The annoyance is a factor.
>
> 3rd We must secure claims that are necessary to us, owned by these people and out of litigation.
>
> 4th Being cleared of litigation our property is in better shape to be disposed of should we desire to do so.
>
> 5th It is prudent to keep from exposing all our workings from becoming accessible to the entire public, as maps, models, testimony and expert examinations would do.
>
> 6th If these suits prevent us from erecting our works this summer, to be able to produce by Jany 1st 1891. We thereby lose very valuable time and opportunities, which may not be compensated by 100 to 200 thousand dollars. So taking it all in all, it is wiser for us to compromise even if our pride suffers."[48]

Evidently, Reed was not sufficiently impressed. In October 1890, the owners of the Mammoth mine offered to sell their properties at prices which he refused. In 1892, he sold his interest in the Bunker Hill and Sullivan while litigation was still pending. Reed's failing health, the suits against the mine, and its financial problems finally convinced Reed to sell out in order to salvage what he could from his investment.[49]

Successful entrepreneurs minimized such problems by consolidating their holdings with those of the opposition in a compromise settlement. Just as the fear of litigation could produce precautionary consolidation, so could a compromise bring about consolidation. A controversy over apex rights between the Northland and Mayflower mines of Park City, Utah, was settled in 1893, after several years of litigation. Kearns, Keith, and their partners purchased the Northland and consolidated it with their other properties. A suit against their Silver King mine, charging the illegal extraction of ore, was comprised in 1907, when the contending forces joined to form the Silver King Coalition Mining Company. In Leadville and Aspen, Colorado, attempts to apply the apex principle, which had been established for fissure veins, to horizontal flat veins occasioned lengthy and expensive suits which were eventually compromised. Silver deposits there sometimes were found in horizontal flat veins which varied from a few inches to a foot in thickness. Separated from each other by deep layers of barren rock, these veins were known as blanket or contact lodes.[50] They were appropriate for location under the principle that the underground boundaries of a claim were the downward extension of the surface boundaries. Wheeler apparently developed the Emma and Aspen mines on this basis until owners of the Durant mine brought suit, claiming the apex rights to his mines. The *Aspen Times* for August 26, 1885, defined the controversy:

The apex racket is to be started again. The people of Pitkin County cannot afford to allow the fissure vein law [1872], which was enacted when flat veins were unknown, to be applied to the contact lode of the mineral belt between Elk Mountain and the Frying Pan. Three hundred by fifteen hundred feet is enough mining ground for anyone. There is no law on the statute books which will allow one who holds the outcrop of a contact lode to take the whole country adjoining.[51]

The aptly named Compromise Mining Company emerged in 1887 as the consolidated product of the litigation. The original properties in the suit were still independently owned but were henceforth operated under practically one management.[52]

Thus, bonanza kings unable to avoid or to win suits over contested title found compromise and consolidation preferable to defeat. A timely consolidation avoided the excessive cost, corruption, and instability of disputed ownership and the litigious apex ruling.[53] More important, it produced the legal security essential for the long-term development of mines and claims.

The entrepreneur unable or unwilling to compromise was wise to sell out as soon as possible. The timing of his decision was crucial, for capitalists were especially reluctant to invest in a mine with a history of contested titles. Reed realized the value of a clear title. In a letter of 1876 to his attorney responsible for purchasing the Sleeper and Conner Creek gold mines in Baker County, eastern Oregon, he said, "If there are to be law suits and conflicting titles to contend against I don't want anything to do with either of the properties."[54] Had Reed sold the Bunker Hill and Sullivan before its lengthy litigation, he would probably have received a greater return on his original investment.

As a promoter and developer of mines in southeastern Nevada, Hearst was quick to dispose of those which became embroiled in litigation. The Eureka was a case in point. The mine had a gross yield of nineteen million dollars and paid over five million in dividends between 1871 and 1881. However, it became involved in a legal battle with the Richmond from 1877 to 1881, and Hearst decided to sell his interest. As he explained, "Those inside got to quarreling. They said we were stalling. I got mad and sold out."[55] In Pioche, near the Eureka district, he invested in mines, until litigation once again advised a timely sale. Of his Pioche activities he said, "I didn't do much, just knocked around a little. Got in with some men who had a set of . . . mines, sunk a shaft, struck a bed of ore, had a big lawsuit over it, got out of that making two hundred and fifty thousand."[56]

Just as depression was the best time for the mining entrepreneur to buy, so prosperity was the most appropriate time to sell. A mine in bonanza attracted buyers, as the members of the San Francisco "bank crowd" well knew. Sharon, for example, demonstrated a shrewd sense of timing when liquidating his stock. "He always sold when prices were high. But he *never* sold when they were at the highest. He left that burden of guessing when the top would be reached to [the] luckily minded."[57] Good timing was not unique to the bonanza kings. When Sheedy was in the cattle business, it was said that he "always finds the dearest market when he buys, and the highest market when he sells."[58] Of course, even the most careful businessmen could guess wrong. Horace Tabor kept the Matchless mine long after it should have been sold, and Jesse Knight went into debt with some of his properties after failing to dispose of them opportunely. However, Knight wisely and profitably sold his first mine, the Humbug, the basis of his fortune, shortly before it played out. He had discovered the mine with the alleged help of divine guidance. This story reportedly inspired the disappointed purchaser, Simon Bamberger, to remark, "Jesse Knight might not have had a revelation when he found the mine, but he surely had one when he sold it."[59]

Adolph Sutro's liquidation of stock in his Comstock tunnel is, perhaps, the best example of a strategically timed sale. The Sutro Tunnel was completed in 1879. Its stock was in demand. It was expected that the discovery of new bonanzas would make the tunnel invaluable. However, at this time, many Comstock mines were declining, and Sutro wisely sold most of his stock for $709,012.50. Those who bet on the revival of the lode were disappointed. Although the tunnel proved useful for drainage, it was completed too late to be of maximum use to mining. Ore bodies extended deep into the earth where the tunnel could be of service, but their low-grade value soon made them unprofitable to work. Moreover, no sizable bonanzas were found after the tunnel began operation. Sutro sold out just in time, receiving more money for his stock than could have been realized at any later period.[60] Sam Davis, the Nevada newspaperman, complained, "It makes me sad, in common with all other old Nevadans to think that any man ever got out of the State with that much money."[61]

Sutro, like most bonanza kings, was sensitive to the opportunities and the limitations created by an unstable industry. Success depended, in part, upon one's ability to exploit those opportunities while preventing the limitations from ruining one's business. The periodic boom-to-bust cycle of mining regions and camps enabled the shrewd entrepreneur to buy when the prices of properties were low and to sell when they were high. A careful, knowledgeable purchase and efficient consolidation were designed to keep these prices high and his properties free of litigation. If or when litigation threatened, the entrepreneur relied on certain corrupt tactics to defeat the opposition or to force a suitable compromise. A compromise was often the most expedient means of legally securing his property, for political tactics were not always reliable and imperfect mining laws and prolonged disputes over title intensified the instability which was naturally a part of the industry. If compromise was not feasible, the mine owner was best advised to heed the warning of litigation and dispose of his holdings. A decline in either the market price of such precious metals as silver or in the production of his mine also made a sale advisable. By following the above strategy, miners made the acquisition, consolidation, and liquidation of claims and mines timely and systematic and were able to overcome the natural and legal instability of the industry.

FIVE

LABOR: CONFLICT AND CONSENSUS

CONTESTED OWNERSHIP and the exhaustion of mineral
resources invariably made business hazardous for the
bonanza king. His workers could create another kind of
instability. Perhaps the most dramatic evidence of dis-
order on the trans-Mississippi frontier has been presented by serious students and popularizers of labor-
management relations in the western mining industry.
Their accounts have often emphasized conflict. Violent
strikes in Colorado and Idaho, the emergence of the
militant Western Federation of Miners, and the federation's organization of the "revolutionary" Industrial
Workers of the World are frequently discussed. Vernon
Jensen's scholarly and aptly named synthesis, *Heritage
of Conflict: Labor Relations in the Nonferrous Metals
Industry up to 1930*, primarily identifies the industry
with labor exploitation and unrest. A standard interpretation of major western mining strikes during the 1890s
creates the impression of mutual hostility between labor
and capital. Unyielding employers recruited deputy
sheriffs, armed guards, and strikebreakers and harassed
striking miners with credit boycotts and beatings. The
result often was a small-scale war between organized
capital and militant labor.[1]

Popular accounts of frontier conflicts between vigilantes and outlaws, homesteaders and cattlemen, and
soldiers and Indians perhaps make it inevitable that
labor-management relations should be similarly char-

acterized. Indeed, such incidents of lawlessness and violence as Harry Orchard's dynamite murder of former Idaho governor Frank Steunenberg, who had used federal troops to break the 1899 Coeur d'Alene strike, undoubtedly contribute to the general impression of unrest and radicalism among western industrial miners.[2] While one cannot underestimate the existence and intensity of labor-management disputes, it is important that they be put into proper perspective. Did leading mining entrepreneurs, the bonanza kings, frequently experience similar disputes? An examination of this question should help to determine the extent of instability in the industry and the labor priorities, policies, and attitudes of the most financially successful western mining capitalists.

During the period under examination, the years from 1892 to 1904 were particularly marked by industrial conflict in mining, as well as in other industries. The strike at the Homestead, Pennsylvania, works of the Carnegie Steel Company in 1892 and the strike against the Pullman Palace Car Company near Chicago in 1894 are notable examples. In 1894 alone 1,400 industrial strikes were called in the nation, involving more than 500,000 workers.[3] Such mining camps and districts as Leadville, Cripple Creek, and Telluride in Colorado and Coeur d'Alene in Idaho experienced violent disputes. Immediate causes varied from labor-management disagreements over the eight-hour day and a minimum-wage scale to the commercial monopoly of company-owned towns.

Identical or similar issues had caused problems before, but in the 1890s these issues were debated in an atmosphere which made them especially irreconcilable. The depression, the repeal of the Sherman Silver Purchase Act, and the steady decline in the price of silver forced owners to suspend operations temporarily, reduce the cost of labor, or, at times, default on the payment of wages. Such efficient technological innovations as the power drill and the cyanide process of treating gold ore reduced some previously skilled workers to unskilled laborers.[4]

The national movement toward corporate organization and consolidation, exemplified by the creation of the Amalgamated Copper Company and the American Smelting and Refining Company in the mining industry, gave owners the concentrated power to resist the demands of organized labor. More important, perhaps, business consolidation brought home to the individualistic miner his comparative powerlessness. Formerly independent prospectors were forced to adjust to the uncomfortably permanent status of wage earners. In the 1890s, miners rebelled against their declining status.[5] How did some bonanza kings react to "rebellion"? An examination of a typical industrial conflict should reveal the tactics used to restore stability.

The Coeur d'Alene labor war of 1892 is an appropriate example. It precipitated the organization of the Western Federation of Miners, which, during its first four years, 1893–96, "seemed a rather ordinary trade union" willing to work within the system and to affiliate with the American Federation of Labor.[6] More important, the Coeur d'Alene conflict reveals the reactions of such bonanza kings as D. O. Mills, a San Francisco mining investor, and particularly John Hays Hammond, the mining engineer, to the demands of organized labor. Mine owners in northern Idaho faced no special problems with their workers until 1887, when a reduction in the wages of car men and shovelers from $3.50 to $3.00 per day in some mines gave rise to unions in the district towns of Wardner, Wallace, Burke, and Gem.[7] Evidently, Simeon Reed was suspicious of what the wage reduction portended. A letter from B. Goldsmith, the acting manager of his Bunker Hill and Sullivan mine, suggested the

need to watch developments among the workers: "I want
the privilege to employ one Confidential man, who quietly and unostentatiously reports to me all about our
employees and about matters concerning our interests
here; there will be much that we can hear through such a
man which otherwise we will not hear."[8]

In 1889, several unions combined to form the first
federation in the hard-rock mining industry, the Coeur
d'Alene Executive Miners' Union. The strength created
by district federation soon became important when the
mine owners installed compressed-air drills, which reduced many skilled miners to unskilled positions as
shovelers and car men at the $3.00 daily wage. Union
members reacted by striking in support of a uniform
ten-hour-day scale of $3.50 for all underground workers.
In 1891, the mine owners accepted the demand, but they
also formed their own organization, the Mine Owners
Protective Association, to restore the old wage scale.[9]

The three major companies in the area, including the
Bunker Hill and Sullivan, owned then primarily by
Hammond, Mills, William H. Crocker of San Francisco,
Cyrus H. McCormick of Chicago, and other eastern
capitalists, were instrumental in creating the new organization, which turned its attention initially to the
railroads rather than to the unions. In late 1891, the
railroads increased their rates on ore shipped to smelters
out of the district by $2. The Mine Owners Protective
Association discontinued operations in protest, thereby
forcing the railroads to restore the previous rates by
March 1892. The association then promised to reopen the
mines if the unions accepted the separate wage scales
which had prevailed from 1887 to 1891 for skilled and
unskilled workers. The unions refused. A similar conflict
over wages had been resolved in Butte much earlier, but
in Coeur d'Alene the opposing sides were less willing to
compromise. Hammond regarded union agitators from

Butte as the source of the trouble. The mine owners also claimed that the low price for silver and lead made wage cuts necessary. Faced with a lockout, the unions found this argument unconvincing and charged the owners with violating previous agreements guaranteeing the $3.50 minimum.[10] The impasse worsened when such employers as Hammond, contrary to state law, imported strikebreakers from California, who were protected behind armed guards and barricades at the mines and mills. When the unions interfered, the owners countered with court injunctions restraining union members from trespassing on mine property, interfering with operations, or intimidating the workers.[11] Injunctions and Pinkerton detectives were favorite weapons of employers insistent upon resuming uninterrupted production in Idaho, Colorado, and eastern industrial centers when labor relations became particularly disruptive. Hammond regarded Charles A. Siringo, who was employed by the Mine Owners Association at Coeur d'Alene to spy on the unions, as "the most interesting, resourceful, and courageous of these Pinkerton detectives."[12]

In July 1892, union members, provoked by the discovery of the Pinkerton spy in their ranks, dynamited the Frisco mill owned by one of the major companies and imprisoned the nonunion workers. Then they took possession of the Bunker Hill and Sullivan concentrator and ordered the superintendent to fire his nonunion employees or see his mill destroyed. Under pressure from the mine owners, the governor declared martial law and sent the state militia and federal troops to restore order.[13] The leading historian of the labor war has remarked that during the "July crisis, the entire machinery of the state power plus the military arm of the federal government were exerted in the owners' behalf."[14] Union members and sympathizers were arrested indiscriminately and imprisoned in stockades at Wallace and Kellogg, although none was ultimately convicted of any crime. Martial law was dissolved in late 1892, under conditions favorable to the employers. An uneasy peace settled over the Coeur d'Alene until 1899, when labor-management relations once again exploded.[15]

Whether one blames the union or the owners for the initial conflict, the incident illustrates the employers' use of political influence and military force to prevent the destruction of property, to keep the cost of hiring armed guards, detectives, and lawyers at a minimum, and to resume operations. Most important, it illustrates the high priority some bonanza kings placed on reducing labor costs in order to achieve success.

The tactics used by mining entrepreneurs to restore law and order during labor strikes at Leadville in 1896, Coeur d'Alene in 1899, and Cripple Creek in 1894 and 1904 generally follow the pattern established during the first Coeur d'Alene conflict. The bonanza kings who were involved in these disputes defined the proper role of organized labor and government in the conservative fashion expected of a typical industrialist of the late nineteenth century.

Hammond was one of the more outspoken commentators on industrial labor relations. As a mining engineer and manager of many enterprises throughout the mountain states, he came in close contact with a type of workingman whose independence made him difficult to handle:

> Though I always kept on friendly terms with workmen, I also understood the point of view of the employer. I early became identified with large corporations and the management of successful companies, and later counted among my friends the great promoters and capitalists of the country. I saw that capital, too, has its rights and minimum wage; that is, the rate of interest as guarantee before the investor can be expected to risk his money in the enterprise.[16]

Hammond supported the right of workers to organize
in order to protect themselves from organized capital,
but he was quick to distinguish between acceptable and
unacceptable unions:

> I believed in the Railway Brotherhoods and also in the American
> Federation of Labor under the guidance of . . . Samuel Gompers. I
> supported both organizations as valuable parts of our industrial
> system. On the other hand, I had no use for the radicalism of the
> I.W.W. [the Industrial Workers of the World organized by the
> Western Federation of Miners in 1905], of which I had had
> experience in the Coeur d'Alene and Cripple Creek. . . . If a gov-
> ernment does not honestly and speedily enforce the laws made to
> protect both individuals and corporate bodies against attacks on
> life and property, it invites disaster upon itself.[17]

During the Western Federation of Miners' strike at
Cripple Creek in 1904, Hammond told a member of
Roosevelt's cabinet that the president should have complied with the Colorado governor's request to send troops
to suppress the "lawless activities."[18]

Evidently, Hammond's mining-engineer colleagues
were even more adamant than he in opposing working-
class radicalism. They viewed the Western Federation of
Miners, which by the turn of the century had broken
with the American Federation of Labor and endorsed a
Marxist-socialist ideology, as a "dictatorial and irrespon-
sible body seeking to overthrow the capitalist system,
and . . . compared the Butte Miners' Union—'a gang of
Irish-Austrian-Italian anarchists'—to the dread Ma-
fia."[19] During an "eight-hour" strike at his plant in 1903,
James B. Grant, a Colorado mining engineer and man-
ager-owner of the famous Omaha and Grant smelter,
charged the Western Federation of Miners with an
insatiable desire to reduce the length of the working day:

> We are in the fight and we'll be there at the finish. What is the use
> of giving in? The Western Federation of Miners now want eight
> hours. If we grant them that it will only be a question of time
> before they are striking for six and if it should get that it will be
> clamoring for four.[20]

Irving Howbert was especially critical of state governments which cooperated with the Western Federation of Miners rather than with the mine owners. In 1893–94, local unions in Cripple Creek became affiliated with the Western Federation of Miners and struck the mines owned by Howbert, David Moffat, and other leading Colorado entrepreneurs who refused to grant the three-dollar, eight-hour day. Cripple Creek soon became an armed camp. According to Howbert, "the striking miners had virtual possession of the camp. They refused to recognize the legally constituted authorities, and by their actions brought about a condition of anarchy that continued for a number of months."[21] The Populist governor of Colorado, David H. Waite, intervened with the militia and settled the conflict on terms favorable to the striking miners. In his memoirs, Howbert objected, "Governor Waite was a most erratic person, thoroughly imbued with socialistic and other fantastic ideas as to matters of government, and had unlimited confidence in his own opinions."[22]

In 1894, Howbert, the chairman of the Colorado State Republican Central Committee, succeeded in getting a Republican who would respect the rights of private property elected to the governor's office and in "redeeming the State from the radical Populistic government" which had supported, among other reforms, the eight-hour day. In Colorado and other western mountain states, Populism was a working-class movement which received support from the Western Federation of Miners.[23] Therefore, such negative terms as *socialism* and *radicalism* which were identified with the Populist movement perhaps were also applied to organized labor.

Some bonanza kings regarded union members as radicals, agitators, or anarchists when they struck for a redress of grievances or became affiliated with the Western Federation of Miners or the Populist party. Such attitudes led to infiltration and repression. Pinkerton spies, injunctions, private and public armies, lockouts, and blacklists became acceptable and effective weapons in the hands of profit-minded owners. By uncompromisingly resisting the demands of organized labor for higher wages and shorter working days, some bonanza kings minimized labor costs and promoted their own success. However, just as labor-management relations could be repressive and violent, so they could be accommodating and peaceful.

Why were not more of the fifty bonanza kings in this study involved in violent or prolonged confrontations with organized labor during the 1890s or even during the 1880s, when mining was already heavily industrialized? Certain explanations are obvious. Labor unrest was not uniformly common throughout the period, nor was it uniformly common in all places. It might well have been that some of the mining moguls, regardless of their labor policies, experienced few problems because their careers were spent primarily in times and places of minimal labor unrest. Those who faced labor discontent undoubtedly realized that attempts to break a strike by force or by deliberately shutting down operations, rather than by immediately negotiating a settlement, could prove expensive. The Cripple Creek strike of 1894, for instance, lasted 130 days, "the longest and bitterest of all American labor disputes up to that time." It cost three million dollars in lost production, lost wages, and upkeep of the armies involved. Moreover, coercive tactics did not always produce lasting stability. The Coeur d'Alene strike of 1899 grew out of the 1892 conflict.[24] The military occupation in 1892 had not destroyed the miners' union. Once again it asserted itself.

These lessons made many entrepreneurs realize that uninterrupted production was preferable to reduced labor costs. Dennis Sheedy acknowledged that a strike at his smelter during the late 1880s had taught him the value of using "kindness with my men." On one occasion he compensated an employee who had lost a leg in a smelter accident by paying his hospital bills and his usual salary during his absence from work and by providing him with one thousand dollars in a final settlement.[25] Sheedy also kept the channels of communication open between labor and management to discourage strikes, saying, "I found that keeping my office open so any man could come to me and talk over his grievances, or make his suggestions for improvement in the smelter, was a good idea; was good for the men and helpful to me."[26]

George Hearst, James B. Haggin, and Lloyd Tevis, the owners of the famous Homestake Gold Mining Company, initiated policies designed to prevent worker dissatisfaction and violence. During the late nineteenth century, the working conditions and the daily wage of $3.50 for skilled miners (and somewhat less for surface workers) at the Homestake properties met with the approval of the local Lead City Miners' Union. The union demand for the eight-hour day in 1906 was accepted by the owners. They also extended credit to workers in order to encourage home ownership, realizing that such a policy most likely would produce serious, hard-working citizens who would not disrupt labor relations. The company built a hospital in 1879 and subsequently adopted a medical-care program for its workers. It also promoted educational facilities and opportunities, in order to attract the stable family man to its employment. Phoebe Apperson Hearst, the wife of George Hearst, was responsible for building and maintaining the Hearst Free Library and the Hearst Free Kindergarten. The Homestake's policies provided superior working conditions and decades of peaceful relations between management and labor, disturbed only once by a lockout unexpected by either side.[27]

Thomas Walsh of Colorado also knew the value of

having satisfied employees. The lessons of worker discontent were evidently in his mind when he wrote to his
partner, David Wegg, in 1894, "As I write our country is
almost in the throes of anarchy. The Pullman strike has
stopped everything, caused riots and bloodshed, especially in Chicago, with millions of dollars worth of property
destroyed, I don't know what we are coming to. You
should rejoice at being both out of office and out of the
country."[28]

Walsh was unwilling to accept the possible consequences of a tough, unyielding policy designed to minimize the costs of labor. His properties were notably free
of strikes. He attributed this situation to a business
philosophy which produced loyal and efficient workers:

> As employers, treat your men with humanity and justice. Provide
> them with clean, comfortable quarters, wholesome food, and keep
> medicines at hand for their use. Money spent for their comfort is
> well spent, for besides the good results in work, you get their
> appreciation and loyalty, which is of incalcuable value.
>
> Strikes can nearly always be averted by having a heart-to-
> heart talk with your men, by fairly and squarely presenting the
> state of the case from their standpoint as well as your own. In
> dealing with them try to get at the best side of their nature. To use
> a mining phrase, you will be prospecting in human hearts and may
> discover beauties of character little suspected.[29]

He put these business maxims into practice by being
one of the first Colorado mining entrepreneurs to adopt
the eight-hour day and by constructing for his Ouray
workers a boarding house, which "housed those having
families as no miners had ever been housed before."[30]

Perhaps local or regional residence, as well as an
awareness of the limitations of a hard-line policy, explains the working-class stability enjoyed by Sheedy,
Walsh, and other bonanza kings. An entrepreneur who
lived or worked near his employees was in a better position to appreciate their problems than one located in a
distant, eastern financial center who visited his mines

only rarely and knew his workers only through a superintendent and impersonal cost sheets.

The fact that the Nevada magnates James Fair and
John Mackay often spent more time underground personally supervising operations than they did above
ground tending to the books helps explain the relative
stability of labor relations on the Comstock Lode.[31] Both
men also maintained family residences in Virginia City,
where their employees lived and worked.

The importance of direct association with employees
was best expressed by the *Miners Magazine* in 1900. In
an article which Big Bill Haywood of the Western Federation of Miners might have written, the magazine
remarked, "The conditions that confront the miner today
are entirely different than the conditions of a quarter of a
century ago, when the mines of the West were owned
largely by individuals who were not too proud or ar-
rogant to live in the same community with their employees."[32]

It is possible to agree with a leading student of labor
relations that the workers in an industry as dangerous
as lode mining resented the determined cost cutting and
profit seeking of absentee owners, who did not see the
results of their policies.[33]

However, an argument which attributes worker exploitation and discontent to absentee ownership over-
looks the fact that such resident western owners as the
Colorado Springs entrepreneurs who confronted rebel-
lious workers at their Cripple Creek properties in 1894,
were at times just as likely to have trouble with their
employees as were absentee eastern owners. The Leadville strike of 1896, for example, occurred when the local
industry was largely under the control of resident owners.[34]

The social and economic background of mining entrepreneurs was a more important determinant of labor

relations than their place of residence or work. Mine owners who had come up from the ranks, having served relatively long apprenticeships as prospectors or practical working miners, often were more benevolent toward their workers than were mine owners who had entered mining as bankers, merchants, or formally educated technicians. Having been wage earners themselves, they could appreciate more fully the grievances of labor than could such financiers with little or no mining experience as Reed, Mills, or Howbert. Therefore, they generally adopted policies which produced satisfied workers and uninterrupted production. Even such thoroughly educated technicians as Grant or Hammond, who had been taught and had personally witnessed the problems of miners, were less than indulgent to labor. Serving primarily as managers of large-scale enterprises, they were often more interested in satisfying profit-seeking investors than in helping the workingmen.

During the Coeur d'Alene conflict in 1892, when Hammond and others discontinued operations, ostensibly to protest increased freight rates, an unknown mine owner who had risen from the ranks confessed to some of his friends among the workers, "You may think the suspension is to secure a reduction in freight rates, but such is not the main issue, and you will find when the mines resume operations, wages will be $3.00 per day for shovelers and car men, and $3.50 per day for miners. I am willing to pay the $3.50 all around, but the rest are not."[35]

Bonanza kings who formerly had been working miners, such as Hearst, Walsh, Winfield Stratton, Thomas Kearns, Mackay, Marcus Daly, Enos Wall, and Jesse Knight, were particularly responsive to the needs of their employees. The policies of Hearst and Walsh have been cited. Stratton of Colorado had been a transient, luckless prospector for seventeen years and a worker in a gold-reduction mill for a brief time before finding success. He could identify with his employees. On one occasion he said, "I am spending fifty thousand dollars a month developing mining property from which I will not take out a cent in ore until the full value of the territory is explored and every cent of that money goes to union labor." He added that he was paying wages of from $3.00 to $5.00 a day when he could hire men for one-half those rates but that he did not think it "right for a former workingman to take advantage of the necessities of his fellow men."[36]

During the Cripple Creek strike of 1894, when other mine operators demanded a ten-hour day or eight hours' work for $2.50 instead of the prevailing $3.00, Stratton signed a compromise scale of $3.25 for nine hours' underground work at his Independence and Portland mines. While the other major mines were shut down, Stratton's continued to operate until an invasion of his properties finally turned him against the strikers.[37]

Previous experience as a miner partially accounts for Kearns's beneficent labor policies. He had learned the trade as an employee of the Ontario Mining Company in Park City, Utah, during the 1880s. When the price of silver fell from eighty-three cents per ounce in 1892 to fifty-four cents in 1897 and forced many mines to close, entrepreneurs in Park City demanded a reduction in wages. The cooperation of all the mine owners was required to make this plan successful. A delegation supporting the wage cut called on Kearns and his partner David Keith, another former mine laborer. They refused to cooperate. Kearns said, "Wages will not be cut with my consent. Our miners are earning all they are being paid, and the mines are making enough to warrant the present wage scale."[38] He also complied with his employees' request to write the eight-hour day into the Utah state constitution. As a delegate to the constitutional

convention in 1896, he was partly responsible for securing the eight-hour day for those engaged in public works
and for instructing the legislature to pass laws providing
for the health and safety of employees in factories,
smelters, and mines.[39]

He instituted an employees' benefit system at his
Silver King mine which embodied most of the best fea-
tures of the workmen's compensation laws long before
Utah had such legislation. In addition, he was always
involved personally in the welfare of his employees.[40]
When hard times brought operations to a temporary
halt, men who had worked longest in the camp or had
families to support were the last to be laid off.[41] His
policies kept the Silver King and his other enterprises
notably free from the devastating strikes of the 1890s.

Mackay, a former California placer miner, day laborer,
timberman, and shift boss on the Comstock, understood
the problems of his workingmen. Although Mackay's
strong faith in self-reliance and hard work did not allow
him to accept easily the collective protest of a strike, he
never forgot that he had once been a working miner.[42]
During periods of declining production on the Comstock
when other mine owners tried to reduce the prevailing
$4.00 daily wage to $3.50, Mackay insisted that economy
should be achieved in some other way. "I always got $4 a
day when I worked in these mines, and when I can't pay
that I'll go out of business."[43] This kind of commitment
encouraged loyalty from his employees and helped him
to stay profitably in business.

Daly's labor policies were also formed by past experience. During the 1860s and 1870s, he had worked as a
placer miner in California, as a lode-mining laborer,
timberman, and foreman in Nevada, and as a superintendent in Utah and Montana. He maintained personal
contact with friends from his laboring days, contributing
to the support of some and bringing others to Butte,

Montana, where he helped them find employment. He was popular with his employees. He took a personal interest in their welfare and paid higher wages than were current.[44] As the manager and part owner of the Anaconda Copper Mining Company, he conceded the right of his workers to strike:

> That is your privilege in this free country. . . . I will see that none of your wives or children suffer until the men can get work again. I have been a working man all my life and know how hard their lot is sometimes. I cannot grant your demands; because it would be an injustice to my company, to the men who have invested millions of dollars here, and besides I am boss here and do not propose to divide my duties with you, but personally I will do all I can for those dependent upon your work.[45]

Daly's honest concern perhaps won the respect even of striking miners.

Wall, who had experienced the rigors of the pick and shovel since the 1860s in such mining areas as Colorado, Montana, Utah, and Idaho, was genuinely sympathetic with the problems of the underground miner. As an investor and superintendent in Idaho's Wood River Valley during the 1880s, he refused to reduce wages at his Wood River Gold and Silver Mining Company properties. Faced with a depressed market for lead and silver, other superintendents in the district had cut wages to $3.50 per day. Colonel Wall maintained the $4.00 rate "even though the reduction would have netted him more than one hundred dollars per day." According to his biographer, "Wall defended the four-dollar day . . . because he was a miner as well as an investor."[46]

Knight was also interested in the miner's welfare. His concern arose from his Mormon faith, as well as from his experience in hauling ore and prospecting in Utah's Tintic mining district during the 1870s and 1880s. At Knightsville, the community which he built in 1897 to service his Tintic properties, Knight attempted to en-

force Mormon standards of morality. He discharged
employees who spent their wages for liquor, neglected
their families, or lived wasteful, licentious lives. He also
closed his mines on Sunday to allow his employees, all of
whom were Mormons, to attend church and compensated
them for the loss of a day's work by raising daily wages
twenty-five cents. This decision prompted the mine operators of the state to drop him from their organization.
Knight did not run a boarding house which employees
were required to patronize, as did other entrepreneurs in
communities that were owned or controlled by mining
companies.[47] He took special care to provide for the
health and safety of his workers. In 1908, he instructed
his superintendent at Eureka, Utah, to be especially
careful of mine accidents:

> I enclose herewith circular letters to be delivered personally to
> each and every ass't, including shift bosses in our employment and
> under your direction. The letters are sent out with the hopes that
> it will bring forcefully to the minds of every man in authority, the
> necessity of giving the very closest attention to all details that will
> minimize accidents to men in our employment.[48]

In 1909, he paid the medical bills and one-half the
monthly salary of a worker who was hospitalized during
September.[49] Knight's paternalism created a spiritual
and economic environment in which tensions between
labor and capital could be minimized.

Thus, many successful mine owners realized that it
was wise to treat their employees respectfully and hu-
manely. Benevolent policies, whether informed by the
lessons of worker discontent, working-class experience,
or religious doctrine, prevented the violent strikes and
sabotage which disrupted the enterprises of other bonanza kings. Employees who were given safe working
conditions and satisfactory wages, hours, housing,
schools, and medical care were more inclined to be efficient and loyal workers than those who were not. If the

mine owner's authority was exercised fairly and respon-
sibly, it could pay rich economic and even spiritual
dividends. Walsh was not the only entrepreneur who
"prospected in human hearts." Nonetheless, beneficent
labor policies were not determined solely by economic or
moral considerations. At times, ulterior political motives
affected the relations of capital and labor.

Politically active or ambitious mine owners with large
labor forces could take advantage of their workers'
voting power. In effect, these owners could become minor
political bosses, exchanging economic favors for political
allegiance or using their control of the job market to
induce their employees to support preferred issues or
candidates. The owners of the Homestead Mining Company apparently gave marked sample ballots to their
employees so they would vote as the company desired.[50]
Such tactics sometimes strained the relations between
labor and management.

If a mine owner personally aspired to high political
office, he was well advised to court, rather than to coerce,
his workers. The benevolent labor policies of Kearns, the
United States senator from Utah, 1901–1904, undoubtedly were influenced by political motives. During his
successful campaign for the Senate in 1872, John P.
Jones, one of the Comstock kings, adopted the eight-hour
day at his Crown Point mine in order to win the labor
vote. Before his decision, the Comstock miners' unions
had been unable to secure the eight-hour day. William
Sharon, a rival mine owner and senatorial candidate,
quickly adopted the practice, and it soon spread throughout the district. Having been elected by the Nevada
State Legislature in 1873, Jones remained in the Senate
for thirty years. His ability to win reelection consistently
can be attributed, in part, to the support of the mine
workers.[51]

The political war between the Montana copper kings

aptly illustrates the mutual dependence of labor and capital. Daly and William A. Clark, the two largest holders of mining property in Butte, occupied center stage in the struggle. Personal incompatibility and economic competition made them bitter political enemies. From 1888 to 1898, Daly was repeatedly successful in thwarting Clark's campaigns for territorial delegate to Congress and for U.S. senator. By attending to the needs of his workers, Daly created moral and political debts, which he collected at election time. Clark's eventual election to the Senate in 1899 was achieved by extensive bribery and fraud. A senatorial investigation, which Daly allegedly helped to finance, exposed the corruption, and Clark resigned.[52]

In 1900, with Daly near death, Clark's political future brightened. He and another prominent Montana mining entrepreneur, F. Augustus Heinze, formed a political alliance. Heinze was engaged in innumerable lawsuits with the Anaconda Copper Mining Company over contested property and desired the election of smpathetic judges. Clark wanted control of the Democratic state convention and the election of a state legislature responsive to his Senatorial ambitions. In a successful move to win labor's support, both men introduced the eight-hour day at their mines and smelters at the prevailing $3.50 wage for ten hours work. After a popular campaign against the Standard Oil–controlled Anaconda, which opposed the eight-hour day, Heinze's judges were elected in the Butte district, and Clark secured the legislature's pledge to send him to the Senate. In 1901, he was duly installed.[53]

Intense political competition in Butte during the late 1880s and the 1890s had created a situation in which the mine owners and their workers could be of service to each other. While the "wars of the copper kings" lasted, workers were given special consideration. They received the eight-hour day, bonuses, turkeys, and other favors. Union officers were given leases on rich ore bodies. In exchange, union leaders and members sold votes and personal services. This mutually beneficial arrangement generally produced harmonious relations between rival owners and their workers in the Butte Miner's Union. However, by 1905, Anaconda had emerged victorious from the war of the copper kings. The ensuing decade saw the destruction of the union.[54]

Conflict and consensus between owners and their workers coexisted in the western mining industry during the last decades of the nineteenth and the first decade of the twentieth centuries. Some bonanza kings preferred to cut labor costs and relied on military and judicial power to enforce and defend their policies. They chose the stick over the carrot as the most effective means of promoting their own success. Their tactics were similar to those of eastern entrepreneurs, like Henry Clay Frick, who used Pinkerton detectives and the state militia to break the Homestead steel strike in 1892. Martial law and the denial of civil rights usually followed serious strikes in the West as in the East.

However, recognizing that a hard-line policy could sometimes result in a considerable loss of life and property and could build a heritage of conflict between workers and owners, other western mining entrepreneurs adopted policies to prevent rather than to suppress the grievances of organized labor. Previous mining experience, moral and religious persuasion, and political expediency fostered benevolence and paternalism.

The bonanza kings who followed this approach usually built a lasting consensus with their workers and, therefore, achieved maximum uninterrupted production. Their attitudes and practices suggest that labor exploitation and instability in the industry have been overemphasized. Indeed, literature on the company-owned mining towns in the twentieth-century West has accentuated the paternalism of employers.[55] Undoubtedly, many bonanza kings agreed with the colorful Colorado mining magnate Horace Tabor when he said, "The labor question has got to be handled by legislative acts and be reached by arbitration. Capital and labor cannot afford to be fighting one another all the time. . . . Their interests are mutual."[56]

Six

CAPITAL AND TECHNOLOGY: BUSINESS ALLIANCES

EDUCATION AND PREVIOUS OCCUPATIONS provided a useful apprenticeship for the bonanza kings. Jobs as bankers, merchants, mine workers, and superintendents and formal or independent study of mineralogy, geology, engineering, or metallurgy produced the capital and technological expertise to enter large-scale industrial mining. However, most entrepreneurs had not acquired sufficient capital and technical knowledge on their own to develop and to sustain successful enterprises. They had to supplement the advantages of their early careers by forming alliances with others who could do for them what they could not adequately do for themselves.

To secure capital, prospective mining magnates formed partnerships and corporations, promoted or publicized their properties, and attracted outside investors. However, at times, investors were victimized by the excessive printing, assessment, and manipulation of stock. Some unscrupulous bonanza kings followed this road to short-term, speculative profit.

Most chose a less unpredictable, more painstaking route and found that technicians were their most important business allies. Whether working as public officials or on their own, academically and practically trained technicians became promoters, advisers, superintendents, general managers, and part owners. They helped to market the stock, improve the equipment and operations, and share the administrative responsibilities

87

of mining enterprises. They were indispensable to entrepreneurs who were primarily financiers, but even entrepreneurs with considerable mining experience and training found them valuable employees and allies. When capital was managed carefully and systematically under their direction or advice, long-term developmental profit could be realized.

The prospector or placer miner could carry on his work with a pick, a shovel, a pan, and a grubstake. Large-scale, deep-level mining required a much greater capital investment, as was realized dramatically upon discovery of the Comstock Lode.[1] According to the old Mexican adage, it required a gold mine to open a silver mine.[2] Gold often existed by itself, but silver usually was found in combination with additional metals. A considerable investment was necessary to mine other ores as well. Properties had to be purchased, and titles had to be maintained by annual exploratory work. Ore had to be extracted, transported, and reduced. Extraction usually demanded hoisting, pumping, drilling, and tunneling machinery and exploratory "dead" work, which could go on for a long time before the mine produced. Low-grade ores were particularly expensive to transport. They frequently had to be concentrated to reduce their bulk and to remove impurities before shipment to distant smelters or refineries sometimes as far away as Wales. Smelting and refining were costly. Complex or refractory ores had to be heated and mechanically or chemically treated to separate the precious or commercially valuable metals from their less marketable companion metals. The entire lode-mining process from the purchase of promising properties to the manufacture of silver or gold bullion or copper products required an investment which was beyond the reach of the individual prospector.

How could aspiring bonanza kings acquire the necessary capital? Such prosperous bankers or merchants as William A. Clark or Jerome B. Wheeler sometimes were able to finance their own enterprises. Other entrepreneurs were favored by inheritance or special benefactions. The organization of the Montana Ore Purchasing Company was made possible by the "considerable fortune" left F. Augustus Heinze and his brothers upon their father's death in 1891. The company built a smelter to service Butte's small independent mines and thereby established a foothold in the district which Heinze later unscrupulously expanded.[3] James B. Grant also profited from family assistance. After financing his nephew's education at Iowa State College, Cornell University, and the School of Mines at Freiberg, Grant's uncle put $300,000 at the young man's disposal. In 1878, the Grant smelter was constructed at Leadville, and the Freiberg graduate was installed as manager.[4]

Most prospective entrepreneurs could not rely on a rich father or an indulgent uncle. If they had been predominantly prospectors or mine workers during their early careers, they were often forced to borrow or to form partnerships in order to accumulate sufficient capital. Jesse Knight had to wait ten years before he was able to develop the Humbug, his first mining claim. In 1896, he secured a loan of $1,500 by mortgaging his ranch near Payson, Utah. According to his son, the second shipment of ore to the United States Smelting Company returned over $11,000.[5] Successive shipments continued to pay for the loan many times over. John Mackay, James Fair, James Flood, and William O'Brien formed a partnership in 1868 to gain control of the Hale and Norcross. Flood and O'Brien borrowed $50,000 to pay for their share of the stock. Fair promised to cover his quota from future earnings and from his salary as superintendent. Only Mackay had enough cash to pay for his three-eighths interest.[6] As on the cattleman's frontier, so on the mining frontier, the partnership was a common early means of acquiring capital.

Partners often minimized the risks and the amount of their investment by taking a bond or option on properties. Purchase of a bond at a fraction of the mine's selling price prevented an unwise, expensive purchase by giving the holder a specified time to investigate or work the property before deciding to buy. Thomas Kearns, David Keith, and their associates bonded the Silver King mine in October 1891 before purchasing it the following summer for $65,000.[7] In 1894, Thomas Walsh informed his partner, David Wegg of Chicago, that he intended to do the same with certain Ouray properties:

> I am giving considerable attention to finding a good mine here and have taken several bonds and options. One mine the "Washington" promises fair. We practically started in July 1st and it payed its own way last month. You and I have control of it. Our first payment commences on Sept. 1st and goes on every 60 days for a year until paid for. Our portion will be $14,000.[8]

If an investor did not want to risk purchasing a promising but unpredictable property, he often took a lease. In 1894, Walsh and Wegg contracted to lease the Ben Butler mine of Colorado for two years.[9] Leases also earned royalties and thereby allowed owners who were short of capital to maintain their properties. In 1895, Walsh wrote his partner: "We can lease the Kokomo mines. I would advise doing this as the taxes and insurance on the property comes high. The royalties from a lease will at least meet those charges."[10] Regarding Horace Tabor's investment in the Big Chief Mining Company in Leadville, his manager, John McCombe, wrote in 1892, "You are much better off in the past eighteen months by having your interest worked under lease than working it yourself."[11] Evidently the declining price of silver made it difficult for Tabor to cover the cost of maintenance and production.

The corporation eventually replaced the partnership as the standard form of business organization on the miner's, as well as on the cattleman's, frontier. Possessing the advantage of limited liability and, at times, the right of stock assessment, the corporation was better suited for the financial risks and demands of expanded mining operations than was the less flexible partnership. Entrepreneurs responded to the requirements of large-scale financing by placing the stock of their heavily capitalized corporations on mining exchanges in such cities as Cripple Creek, Colorado Springs, Butte, and, most notably, San Francisco. On the mining frontier, the corporation frequently served as a device for raising capital.

The situation was different in the East. The financial demands of organizing a business did not yet require the assets of countless small investors. The corporate device seldom was necessary for recruiting capital. Most industrial concerns were owned by relatively few individuals. In 1896, only twenty industrial companies listed their shares on the New York Exchange.[12]

Certain western mining corporations assessed their stockholders periodically, especially to finance exploratory work, when a mine was not producing. From 1859 to 1875, assessments on the Comstock's Crown Point mine amounted to $2,575,500, while dividends totaled $11,898,000.[13] Some mine owners regarded assessments as the essence of corporate financing. Knight, for instance, remarked to the superintendent of one of his Utah properties in 1909, "Unless a corporation is so that we can assess it we consider it almost worthless."[14] Assessments on his mines ranged from a half cent to five cents per share, with one cent the most common rate. If

they were not paid, the stock fell delinquent and was
advertized for sale at public auction.[15]

Knight also relied on the sale of treasury stock to
finance operations. In 1907, the stockholders of his Big
Hill Mining Company of Utah were given the opportunity to buy treasury stock at five cents per share in
proportion to the number of regular shares each held.[16]
When this method was being considered to finance
another company, the secretary informed a concerned
investor:

> We have in the treasury of the East Tintic Consolidated Mining
> Company 94,090 shares stock. We have endeavored a number of
> times to dispose of sufficient of this stock to carry on our patent
> work without assessing, but did not feel justified in selling at the
> present market price. The stock in most of the companies in which
> we are interested is assessable whether or not there is treasury
> stock in the treasury. . . . Neither have we ever assumed to boost
> any property to sell treasury stock at fabulous prices for de-
> velopment work. Whenever we have sold treasury stock we have
> taken our proportion at the same price at which the balance has
> been sold to the public.[17]

Owners of mining, milling, and smelting corporations
also were forced to borrow. Knight frequently refused
requests for loans and invitations to invest because he
was borrowing very heavily. He once told a disappointed
solicitor, "It requires a great deal of money to operate
and develop the properties I am working."[18] In 1908, he
had several hundred thousand dollars in notes outstanding at the Zion's Saving Bank and Trust Company
of Utah. Simeon Reed also drew on the banks. In 1891,
he borrowed $60,000 from the First National Bank of
Portland and shortly thereafter, an additional $110,000
from the W. H. Crocker Bank of San Francisco.[19] During
the depression of the 1890s, his secretary advised him to
seek Crocker's help again: "You cannot borrow money
here [Portland], and although I know how much you

dislike to call on Mr. Crocker ... I can see no other course than to go to him for it."[20]

Entrepreneurs borrowed occasionally from the companies with which they did business. The Montana Ore Purchasing Company received several hundred thousand dollars in loans from the Nichols Chemical Company and the American Metals Company, the refining and selling agents for Heinze's enterprise. Samuel Hauser's Helena Mining and Reduction Company, which smelted Reed's ores, extended credit to the Bunker Hill and Sullivan mine on future shipments of concentrates.[21] The procedure whereby smelters advanced funds to contracting mines perhaps was best described by Walsh: "What we do in the way of sampling is to take a grab sample, and the Silverton [Colorado] smelter advances us 75% as shown by this sample. When the machinery at [the] smelter starts it will be sampled and a final settlement made."[22]

Although partners and corporate managers could utilize various techniques for acquiring capital, investors still had to be persuaded to purchase options, leases, and stock, to pay stock assessments, and to advance loans. Therefore, mining enterprises often were promoted by the owners themselves or their agents. Both appealed to outside sources of capital and took advantage of their special connections, reputations, and training.

Mine owners sought especially to attract investors in the eastern United States and in Great Britain. Finding San Francisco capitalists unresponsive, Nevada's White Pine mining district looked to the East in 1869. According to the *White Pine News*, completion of the transcontinental railroad would make eastern capital more accessible:

> When a large share of our mines are owned by Eastern capitalists, as in time they will be, such financial distress as now prevails in

San Francisco will cease to affect us seriously. Our Pacific Metropolis has never afforded the mining regions the amount of capital needed for their development, nor proved a sure reliance for carrying through the mining enterprises initiated by its aid. The railroad having connected us with the greater financial centers of the older States, we may in the future depend upon a more ample, stable and reliable money market.[23]

Some western mining companies were incorporated in New York and in nearby states, in part, to attract outside capital. Only one of the six most prominent mines in Leadville during the early 1880s, the Robert E. Lee, was incorporated locally. Such bonanza kings as Bela Buell and Joseph DeLamar drew heavily upon absentee investors. In 1863, Buell and his partner John Kip organized the Kip and Buell Gold Company in New York City. By 1865, the original company had been reorganized with eastern backing as the Kip and Buell Gold Mining and Tunneling Company of Colorado. During the 1880s, Christian and Louis Wahl, members of a Chicago investment firm, supplied much of the capital to develop and to improve the DeLamar mine and mill near Silver City, Idaho.[24] When financing their enterprises, western mine owners did not conform to the self-reliant, rugged-individualist stereotype frequently associated with the frontier.

Western investment bankers also depended upon outsiders. Hauser, the organizer and owner of the First National Bank of Helena, took advantage of his connections and good credit rating with correspondent banks in New York City and Saint Louis to finance such enterprises as the Helena and Livingston Smelting and Reduction Company.[25]

Hauser functioned more as a full-time professional promoter than as a developer. Unlike most bonanza kings, he was more interested in organizing than in managing or administering mining companies. As a promoter, he persuaded prominent persons to take an interest in the Helena and Livingston Company by offering very attractive terms, including a six-month guarantee against loss of the investment and a special bonus of one common share for each share of preferred stock.[26]

The technique of associating well-known political and social figures with mining companies was a common practice. Anglo-American companies often included members of Parliament and titled gentlemen on their boards of directors or stock subscription lists. These so-called decoy ducks, who frequently were only nominally interested in the companies, attracted the unwary investor. Such American politicians as the two U.S. senators from Nevada, William M. Stewart and John P. Jones, capitalized on their political prestige and contacts when marketing mining properties at home or abroad.[27] In the promotional business, political reputation apparently counted as much as special banking connections.

Knight's reputation as a successful practical miner frequently made advertisements in local mining journals and the services of professional promoters unnecessary.[28] According to a broker from central Utah who inquired about handling his stock, "Its a fact down this way it [is] easier to get people to invest in stocks that he is interested in, for the simple reason I guess, THAT HE HAS MADE GOOD."[29] In 1909, a Chicago brokerage firm informed Knight that his reputation also enticed eastern investors:

> We have a number of customers who are interested in Colorado, Iron Blossom and other of the companies in which you hold the controlling interest, and we are free to say that most of our people were largely influenced in their investments by reason of the fact that you personally control and manage these properties. . . . You are looked upon as a practical miner and not as a stock manipulator.[30]

The business reputation of property holders perhaps was

as important as their properties in attracting capital. Nonetheless, prospective investors usually demanded an examination and a favorable report by a technical expert before committing their funds. Such public examinations as those conducted by the U.S. Geological Survey reduced the risks of investment. In 1881, Samuel F. Emmons of the Geological Survey informed Tabor:

> I have seen it stated in the papers that Government ought to do more for the mining interests of Colorado. To show that Colorado has not been neglected I would state that already . . . over $50,000 of Government money has been expended under my supervision, and the results of this work, will it is hoped, be soon put before the Public.
>
> I know you feel a great interest in the development of the mineral wealth of the west and of Colorado in particular and I think you will agree that the work we are doing will accomplish good results toward that end, furnishing accurate scientific data, free from any suspicion of personal bias, not only for Eastern capitalists but in a form that will be thoroughly understood and relied upon in Europe.[31]

The findings of public examiners were supplemented by those of private mining engineers and geologists. Favorable reports were used for public consumption at home or abroad, being quoted in the prospectuses, the handbills, the newspaper advertisements, and the annual reports of mining companies.[32] The promotional role of the formally trained technician is exemplified by a letter N. P. Hill wrote to his wife from Colorado in 1865: "Two different sets of men in Rochester want me to supply them with mining properties. A man in Albany also applies for the same favor. He says he will sell a property if I can recommend it."[33] A similar reason prompted James B. Haggin and the other owners of Utah's Daly mine to retain Joshua E. Clayton. The noted mining engineer's report undoubtedly enhanced the market value of the mine: "If the deep drainage system now in contemplation is carried through to the Daly mine within the next five years, it ought to pay dividends at the present rate, annually for the next 15 or 20 years."[34] Adolph Sutro hired Baron von Richthofen to publicize and to stimulate investment in the Sutro Tunnel. The internationally known geologist testified that the Comstock Lode was a "true fissure vein" and recommended construction of the tunnel. In 1890, Reed offered the Freiberg graduate John Hays Hammond a commission of 2,500 shares if he could find $300,000 to finance a new concentrator and an aerial tramway for the Bunker Hill and Sullivan. Hammond obtained a loan of $150,000 from D. O. Mills, who was also given 50,000 shares as security with an option to buy at $3 a share.[35] Thus, the mining technician was an indispensable worker in the capitalist's campaign to market stock and secure loans.

Successful promotion demonstrated the entrepreneur's ability to bargain on the strength of his reputation and his business connections. If eastern correspondent bankers, prominent politicians, or trained mining experts were included among his business contacts and associates, he usually was able to secure sufficient investment capital. However, capital was not always managed in the best interests of the investor. At times he was the unsuspecting victim of stock speculation and manipulation and of exploitative mine management.

One can only guess how frequently the bonanza kings indulged in these practices. Some emphatically declared their innocence, thereby raising doubts about the methods of others. Walsh insisted that he was not in the "mining stock business" and did not look favorably upon "flotations of property on a stock basis."[36] George Hearst contended that "our mining has been in every way legitimate; that is to say, Mr. Haggin and myself would get a mine, put men to work, put in machinery without regard to any stock. I do not believe that in the Anaconda mine there is a single share sold."[37] Knight informed an inquiring stockbroker, "I am not in the business for keeping stocks up or knocking them down. I simply work for the dividends."[38] Those who gained admission to his mines were not always so honest. In 1909, he remarked, "We invite the fullest investigation of our mines, and mining methods, but we are obliged to be a little careful, because unscrupulous persons have taken advantage of our leniency in the past, and have circulated false rumors, both boosting and knocking our property."[39]

There is more than circumstantial evidence to suggest that the bonanza kings sometimes were "knockers" and "boosters." Even Walsh considered appealing to New York brokers to increase the value of his Ouray properties: "It might be necessary for the New York end to give our stock and perhaps a portion of the treasury stock the entire sway on the N.Y. board until a certain sum was realized." He told his partner of a business associate who "has an outfit that can make the stock very valuable on the . . . exchange provided we can make the earnings justify it at this end."[40] Others were much more unprincipled than Walsh. Tabor, Jerome Chaffee, and David Moffat were all guilty, to a degree, of exploiting Leadville's early mines. It was customary to press rapidly for production of the richest ore in order to reap a harvest of appreciated stock values before selling out.[41] According to a contemporary observer, Chaffee, Moffat, and their New York partners put the stock of the Little Pittsburg Consolidated on the market in 1879 and "cleaned up $2 million in cash before the Little Pittsburg went through. They were not over six months on that deal. . . . It was one of the largest speculative mining transactions in Colorado before or since, and the most successful financial operation, because it was more a financial operation than a mining transaction."[42] Sometimes the mine workers were used unwittingly in fraudulent stock promotion schemes. In 1880, Winfield S. Keyes, the manager of Leadville's Chrysolite mine, provoked a strike in order to cover up the corrupt activities of the principal owner, George D. Roberts, the former San Francisco stock shark who had recently acquired the mine from Tabor. By disrupting production, the strike allowed Roberts and his partners to unload their stock at high prices without exposing the barrenness of the formerly productive mine. When the local miners themselves broadened the strike to advance their own particular interests, the owners fortuitously found increased protection for their corrupt plan. During the strike, one million dollars was received from the sale of overpriced paper.[43]

The excessive assessment of stock to profit insiders was also part of the mining business. A contemporary critic remarked that "the laws of California and Nevada, allowing the officers of corporations to call assessments on mining shares, greatly aided the operators in 'fleecing' small stockholders, and in defrauding them of their rights."[44] By 1885, the Yellow Jacket mine on the Comstock had produced $2,180,000 in dividends, but had levied $2,360,000 in assessments. The nearby Imperial Empire mine had received $600,000 more in assessments than it had paid in dividends.[45]

Perhaps the most flagrant examples of corruption occurred on the Comstock. According to one authority, "it was generally believed that the mines were worked in the interest of the stock speculators rather than the stockholders."[46] Stock values were deliberately depressed by assessments or insinuations of mismanagement, enabling insiders to buy cheaply and to reap huge dividends from the production of rich ore. The strategy was concealed by keeping the miners underground for days on end. False reports of rich ore also were issued to induce credulous investors to buy worthless stock. After fully exploiting the Savage mine in the 1870s, Alvinza Hayward and Jones bid up the price of their stock and sold out at an impressive profit.[47] Thus, the small investor was victimized by bonanza kings who were as interested in mining the stock exchanges as they were in mining the ore.

Consequently, they were accused of deliberate speculation, dishonesty, and waste by those who were knowledgeable of mining technology. Almarin Paul, a careful student of systematic mining, saw three reasons for the frequent failure of mining enterprises: the construction of too much expensive machinery on unproven properties; the expenditure of too much money for corporate speculation and too little for practical mining; and the use of an inefficient system for processing and reducing the ore. He argued that "we must go slower, calculate closer, and work ores better."[48] Geologist Emmons reported that "the occupation of mining, its search after the unseen and unknown, its sudden and unlooked-for vicissitudes, the supposed importance of keeping up an excitement in order to attract capital, have in many cases so biased the moral sense of otherwise honest men that they seem to consider it a duty to themselves and their community . . . to exaggerate the production or value of any mining property."[49] In one of his many speeches as an active member of the Republican party, mining engineer Hammond argued: "Corporations should be judged, not by their magnitude but by their dominant purpose, and their methods, and the manner in which these affect the public welfare. I suggested that federal incorporation or federal licensing would serve to control one of the chief evils of big business: overcapitalization."[50]

Indeed, watered stock, whose total declared value exceeded the real value of the corporation, often was floated to obtain profits for insiders in the mining industry. Some companies honestly overestimated the value of their holdings. Others deliberately tried to deceive the public. For whatever reason, the Little Pittsburg Consolidated Company, the Amalgamated Copper Company, and the American Smelting and Refining Company overcapitalized.[51] On the Comstock, a number of companies took advantage of the rising demand created by a big discovery in one mine by overissuing and overpricing stock in other mines. A contemporary reporter thought the public was as much to blame as the stock speculator:

> The thermometer of values was in the public and not in the mines ... stock speculators have been governed more by the temper of the public than the prospects of the mines. The question is not whether the mine is a safe investment, but whether the market is rising or falling. It is not strange that fortunes were made by a few when the public were so ready to buy at any rates.[52]

Government technicians were especially critical of the Comstock. Clarence King, the first director of the U.S. Geological Survey, regarded the Comstock as a gigantic stock lottery.[53] In 1868, Rossiter Raymond, the federal commissioner of mining statistics, recorded his impressions of the lode:

> All the explorations in the barren mines of the Comstock could have been executed with the money flung away by the mines that have had, for a time, rich ore. ... As the prospects of mining on the old wasteful plan grow darker and darker, officers, agents, and stockholders bend their energies to save what they can by speculation out of the approaching wreck. We might well afford to leave them to their fate, but for the fact that the effect of an abandonment of the Comstock Lode would be almost fatal to systematic and permanent mining in the Pacific States. It would confirm the mischievous feeling that mining is half grab and half gamble; that the only way to make money at it is to dig out what rich ore you can get, and then find a fool to buy the property; or failing that, to make a fool of the collective individual, the public, and to "unload" yourself of your stock.[54]

Eliot Lord, whose monograph *Comstock Mining and*

Miners was sponsored by the federal Geological Survey, blamed the stockholders for mismanagement:

> As a body they have been as greedy as young ravens and fully as heedless, clamoring for dividends without questioning closely the methods of production. If, then, the work of reducing the ore was pressed too rapidly, the mine managers might urge with some force that their action was justified by the accord of the majority of the shareholders, and that mines are necessarily managed to satisfy owners and not economic theories. For the haste with which the ore was extracted no justification is needed.[55]

Some bonanza kings regarded mining, indeed, as "half grab and half gamble." Quick, huge speculative profits were made by overcapitalizing a corporation, attracting stockbrokers and investors, levying excessive assessments, gutting the mine of its richest ore, and liquidating the stock before the roof caved in physically or financially. Such methods were dishonest. They also violated the economic principles of order, efficiency, and marginal utility and strained the alliance between the capitalist and the technician, which had functioned satisfactorily on the promotional level.

However, the bonanza kings usually were more interested in legitimate mining than in stock speculation and manipulation. Therefore, they appealed frequently to government and private technicians as advisers, superintendents, inventors, and managers. A close partnership between capital and technology was necessary for sustained promotion, production, and profit.

When quartz or lode mining first developed, there were no mining bureaus, treatises on vein formation, or descriptions of ores to instruct the entrepreneur. He had to work blindly.[56] Technological problems sometimes forced even the most conscientious entrepreneurs to make mistakes and encouraged stock speculation as a shortcut to profit. State and federal governments sought to eliminate opportunistic stock and mine management by providing useful scientific information to the entrepreneurs. Although some bonanza kings undoubtedly were suspicious of governmental intervention, many welcomed the opportunity to improve their operations.[57]

Government mining agencies and bureaus received political support from entrepreneurs. As a California state assemblyman, 1865–66, Hearst took a special interest in the state's geological survey organized by Joshua D. Whitney in 1860. Hearst sat on the Committee of Mines and Mining Interests which reported favorably on the survey's service to the industry. He also attended a meeting of miners in San Francisco in January 1866, and he voted to endorse the newly organized state mining bureau which was responsible for making assays and collecting ore specimens. Federal agencies also received support. In 1891, fifty mine owners and managers in Aspen, Colorado, were so impressed by the U.S. Geological Survey's examination of Leadville that they petitioned for government geologists to study their mines.[58] In his autobiography, Hammond, who formerly had been employed by the survey, declared: "Although I did no selfish lobbying, I have not hesitated to use what influence I possessed in behalf of adequate financial appropriations for scientific bureaus, such as the Smithsonian Institution, Geodetic Survey, the Geological Survey, and the Bureau of Standards."[59] In 1908, Knight urged his congressman to back a bill creating a U.S. Bureau of Mines: "I think this bureau would be of as great benefit to the mining industry throughout the U.S. as is the Dept. of Agriculture to the farming industry of our country."[60]

Mine owners were especially interested in the work of the U.S. Geological Survey. As originally administered by Clarence King, 1879–81, the survey was primarily a service agency for the industry. It provided detailed geological studies of selected mining districts from which general theories could be formulated regarding the origin and formation of ore deposits.[61] According to the noted mining engineer Thomas A. Rickard, Emmons's monographic study of the Leadville region, published in 1886, taught Rocky Mountain miners "how great was the immediate and practical usefulness of a correct geological diagnosis of a . . . district." At Leadville and Aspen "the financial success of mining operations was dependent largely upon the elucidation of a complex system of faults. This was done by the geologist with a skill that the miner acknowledged with gratitude."[62] Evidently Knight communicated regularly with the U.S. Geological Survey. In 1909, he received the mining production report for 1907 and a map of the western mining districts. Less knowledgeable of mining geology than Knight, Reed had a greater need for technical instruction and advice. In 1887, through the services of the U.S. senator from Oregon, he received a copy of *Mineral Resources of the United States*, published annually by the U.S. Geological Survey beginning in 1882.[63] Acquisitions of technical literature and expressions of political support usually demonstrated the entrepreneur's faith in government technicians and practical, business-minded scientists.

Mining entrepreneurs also depended upon professional, scientific, and technical organizations. Hearst, Heinze, Clark, Walsh, Hammond, and others were members of the American Institute of Mining Engineers, formed in 1871. Hammond was the president of the organization, 1907–1908, and in 1929 received its highest award, the Williams Lawrence Saunders gold medal. Members regularly convened to hear and to discuss papers on the latest mining equipment, metallurgical processes, and related matters. These papers were published as the *Transactions* of the institute. Reed owned many volumes.[64]

Bonanza kings also found membership in other groups helpful. Knight belonged to the Utah chapter of the American Mining Congress. Walsh was a member of the American Association of Mining Engineers, the Washington Academy of Sciences, and the American Association for the Advancement of Science. Hammond listed the American Society of Mechanical Engineers and the British Institution of Mining and Metallurgy among his many affiliations.[65] Grant was an original member of the Colorado Scientific Society, formed in 1882 with the support of the U.S. Geological Survey. This organization, whose members included metallurgists, assayers, chemists, geologists, mining managers, and mining engineers, "brought men of science into contact with those who needed to apply the ideas of science in their daily work."[66] Some bonanza kings may have belonged to these associations for social rather than for professional reasons. Most undoubtedly joined in order to keep informed of new technical and scientific developments, demonstrating the value of cooperation between the capitalist, the technician, and the scientist.

Mining technicians often were entrusted with a large share of managerial responsibility. Therefore, bonanza kings tried to hire the best-qualified men. Experience and efficiency were especially desired in superintendents. In 1887, J. F. Wardner, the manager of Reed's Bunker Hill and Sullivan, evaluated the mine's superintendent: "Jenkins is a capital man, has been with us a year—He knows a mine and is economical—Have no fears on the subject, all is well."[62] Evidently Reed was not satisfied. His quest for a replacement indicates that reliable, talented superintendents were not easy to find. Dell Linderman, the owner of the Commercial Steam Power Works of San Francisco, informed him: "Had you instructed me to send you up the Palace Hotel it would be about as easy a matter as to get the man you want.

[Alvinza] Hayward says it is the ——— hardest thing in
the world to find. . . . You don't want an old Comstock
mining Supt. They would bust an iron globe wide open
and make a mine of solid gold squeal for more mud."[68]
This opinion was not shared by all bonanza kings.
Comstock superintendents frequently were practical
miners who had come up from the ranks and, therefore,
were preferred over formally trained mining engineers.
Hearst was unwilling to hire the young Hammond until
the latter convinced him that he had not learned anything important at Freiberg.[69] Hearst once said, "I think
I may claim to know all about rocks, this knowledge
however I did not obtain from books. It is altogether
practical. . . . There are many people who may be smart
enough and know all that the books can teach them but
when it comes to practically make a use of that knowledge, they are of no account."[70] Dennis Sheedy, the
general manager of the Globe Smelting and Refining
Company, also stressed the advantages of practical experience: "During my term of management I obtained
many letters patent of inventions and improvements,
many of them being in use today. My explanation is that
by studying and by experiments I found the practical
things. I put practical, businesslike ideas into force.
These principles are not taught in technical schools."[71]
Henry Wolcott of the Boston and Colorado Smelting
Company was described as a "practical—mark the word
—miner in the old county of Gilpin" during a guberna-
torial nominating speech at the Colorado state republican convention in 1898.[72] Some bonanza kings regarded
practical experience as politically, as well as profes-
sionally, useful.
      Self-taught practical mining entrepreneurs often re-
sented academically trained mining engineers, whose occasionally supercilious manners and early, costly errors
in judgment were not easily overlooked or forgotten.

Some suffered because the public often judged the bona fide engineers by their imitators.[73] Others were apparently victims of an anti-intellectualism which affected even engineers like Hammond, although he had the reputation of being a "genuine mining man, practical and sensible."[74] In a conversation with a Yale colleague in 1903, Hammond objected to being called professor. "That is all right, to call me professor at a [faculty] meeting. But as soon as I leave the meeting I am no longer professor. . . . Because a professor in mining is looked on with high contempt and suspicion by the practical engineers of the country."[75]

Although criticized and resented, "them damned eddicated fellers" were too valuable to ignore.[76] Even practical miners grudgingly utilized their services. Marcus Daly, for example, reportedly said, "I listen to the reports of my engineers and then I lock myself in my room lest they influence my judgment."[77] During the 1870s, Mackay and Fair employed W. H. Patton, a civil and mechanical engineer, to design and construct the stamp mills and the hoisting and pumping machinery at their mines. Mining financiers also needed the college-educated technician. In the 1880s, Wheeler hired Walter B. Devereux, a graduate of the Columbia School of Mines, to take charge of his Aspen smelter. Haggin retained practical miners and trained engineers on his payroll, engaging the former to examine properties and the latter to develop and operate them.[78] By the 1890s, most bonanza kings undoubtedly had employed both practically and formally trained technicians as consultants and superintendents.

Regardless of their educational and professional backgrounds, mining technicians ultimately were selected for their performance on the job. Most bonanza kings, and particularly mining financiers, chose their technicians wisely. According to Henry Wolcott, "Moffat's success

[was] the result of his associating himself with the right man. . . . He [was] a pretty fair judge of human nature."[79] William Sharon and Mills were similarly gifted. According to a witness, Sharon lived on the Comstock "as the representative of the Bank of California . . . I doubt if Mills was ever underground a dozen times in his life. . . . They were investors, with no yen for underground work so manifest in some. But Mills and Sharon were good judges of men and selected clever ones to do their mining for them."[80] Such practical mining entrepreneurs as Hearst also were adept at hiring talented technicians. While a part owner of the Ophir Company on the Comstock, he employed Philip Deidesheimer. The Freiberg graduate invented the revolutionary technique of square-set timbering. Interlocking hollow cubes built of heavy timber were placed in tiers one above another. When filled with waste rock, they were able to support the enormous Comstock ore bodies without the danger of cave-ins. A contemporary reporter acknowledged the importance of the innovation: "It was a necessity. The mines could have been worked by no other plan. With it the miners could safely extract ore to any height, or any width, or any length, or any depth. Without it they could do nothing or next to nothing."[81] After the invention in 1860, the practice spread to such other camps and districts as Butte where it facilitated the deep-level mining of other large ore bodies.

Other innovations facilitated the extraction of ore. Open-cut methods using steam or electric shovels to strip away and load the raw ore into railroad cars helped make profitable mass mining of low-grade porphyry copper. Daniel Jackling, an inventive mining engineer, helped develop the open-cut or block-caving technique which was used at Bingham Canyon by Samuel Newhouse and Enos Wall of the Utah Copper Company.[82] The technician improved mine management as well as mine engineering. In particular, he sponsored better planning and greater exploratory development.[83] This was especially necessary after the mines had been relieved of their richest ore. Sam Jones, the experienced, practical superintendent of his brother's Crown Point mine, recognized the marginal utility of low-grade quartz and waste material used to fill square-set cribs. A careful, systematic sorting and reworking of this marginal ore not only returned a slight profit but also led to the discovery of new ore veins during the late 1880s and the early 1890s. Jones's interest in maximizing production was acknowledged by a witness: "It was due to his intelligence, his persistence, his courage, that the second revival of the Comstock occurred."[84]

The technical expertise of the specialist was most in demand when the ore was reduced. DeLamar hired Jackling to develop a large-scale cyanide plant for treating gold and silver ores at his Mercur, Utah, properties. The plant was the first to use powdered zinc on a commercial scale as a precipitant for cyanide solutions.[85] In 1898, the owners of the Homestake Mining Company gave a five-year contract to Charles W. Merrill, a graduate of the University of California, Berkeley, and an expert in cyanidation, to devise a method of saving a higher percentage of the value of gold ore than was achieved by the amalgamation process. In 1899, a sixty-ton experimental plant to work the tailings was built. By 1902, the amalgamation and cyanide processes together were saving 88 percent of the ore's value, an increase of 18 percent over the previous recovery method.[86]

Complex or refractory ores usually required smelting. As described by mine superintendent Victor Clement, the operation demanded the services of the trained technician:

> The art of smelting consists in effecting desirable chemical interchanges or reactions to bring the metal in view in a more con-

centrated or marketable form. The chemical constituents are what govern any smelting problem. Generally, the object in view is to eliminate, in the cheapest way possible, the non-marketable constituents of an ore. This is effected by forming slags—equivalent to tailings. In order to form these slags, definite ratios of silica, iron, lime, sulphur etc have to be employed. Nearly in every case, the ore itself of a mine will contain one or more of the important ingredients for its own fluxing or slagging. The question resolves itself to supplying those wanting.[87]

Hill hired Richard Pearce and Herman Beeger, formally trained metallurgists, as advisers and supervisors for his Boston and Colorado Smelting Company. When Thomas Egleston of the Columbia School of Mines examined the company's Blackhawk plant in 1874, he reported that the silver bars produced were "999 to 999.5 [percent] fine."[88] The purity of the final product testifies to the efficacy of the smelting and refining process. Much credit goes to Pearce, who developed the refining method by which the precious metals were separated from the copper.[89]

Communication with government agencies and membership in professional, scientific, and technical organizations undoubtedly made the owners of mining properties receptive to the technical innovations of their carefully chosen superintendents and advisers. However, the bonanza kings usually were not bold risk takers. As the most easily worked and richest ores were exhausted, they paid more attention to Paul's advice to "go slower, calculate closer, and work ores better."

New techniques and new equipment were adopted conservatively. Knight was careful to buy only proven machinery. In 1909, he wrote the manufacturer of a newly designed drilling machine: "I am not convinced of the success of the drilling machine. . . . Until this machine has done something more than experimental work, I would not care to take any chances other than the letting of a contract [i.e., to run a tunnel]."[90] The owners of the

Homestake Company were equally cautious. They were not pioneers in the industry, but rather copiers of methods that had proved successful elsewhere.[91] As owners of the Anaconda Mining Company, Hearst, Haggin, and Daly also were reluctant to implement unproven techniques. In 1887, Reed received a letter from Butte suggesting the value of experimenting before innovating: "I would not build a concentrator like the Bunker Hill and Sullivan have got, but would put in a Steam Stamp and Concentrate by Hydraulic separation—In fact it would well repay you to come here and see the difference in the operations of the Concentrating plants, in and around Butte—The Anaconda Co. have spent lots of money experimenting, and they are doing away with the old process, as the other is much cheaper and does better work."[92] Walsh spent a considerable amount of money in experimental smelting, erecting an iron and copper pyritic smelter at Kokomo, the first in Colorado, and later another at Silverton. The smelters employed the Austin process which had been used previously in Montana. In 1896, Walsh commented that "with an abundance of ores of the right kind I know of no greater money maker."[93] In 1903, he informed a promoter who was trying to sell a new process for reducing refractory ores that he always looked before he leaped: "I have no faith in new processes until they are proven by long continued successful tests —as an investment they don't interest me."[94] Prior use and patient experimental testing were advisable before adopting new processes, methods, or equipment. The bonanza kings, like entrepreneurs in such industries as textiles and iron and steel, were not bold, risk-taking, technological innovators.[95]

The alliance between the technician and the mining capitalist was not one-sided. Each needed the other to maximize production and minimize costs. At times they were partners, sharing the administrative responsibilities of their company. The technician managed the operations in the field, usually with the aid of other technicians, who served as superintendents or as consulting engineers. The capitalist generally took care of the financial, accounting, and sometimes the legal problems of the company. While Fair and Mackay attended to the technical demands of mining and reducing the ore, their partners, Flood and O'Brien, watched the stock market for the best time to buy and to sell. The mutual trust which sustained such an arrangement perhaps is best exemplified by the partnership of Hearst, Haggin, Lloyd Tevis, and Daly. Before Daly joined the firm, Hearst was the chief field manager, examining, purchasing, and operating such properties as he desired. Haggin and Tevis, who were lawyers and financiers, usually deferred to his technical expertise and provided the necessary capital and legal advice.[96] Haggin accorded Daly, a co-owner and the general manager of the Anaconda, similar respect. After examining the company's smelter in 1883, Haggin said:

> The property is bigger than you led me to believe, which I suspected was the truth before I left home; you have shown me where all the money has gone which I was confident I would find.
>
> Indeed, I do not see how you could do the work with so little money, and you tell me what is needed, which is clear enough, but I am no better satisfied than I was before I left home, and so all this work of mine has been useless. Hereafter, please keep in mind what I told you when we first began this enterprise: when you need money draw, and keep drawing.[97]

A similar arrangement was shared by the Heinze brothers. F. Augustus was the mining expert, Arthur was the legal specialist, and Otto Charles, who ran his father's prosperous importing firm, was the businessman. Together they discussed all problems and maintained strict loyalty to each other. In matters of mining, politics, or how a jury would react, the group customarily heeded the advice of F. Augustus. Legal problems were handled by Arthur, and credit was secured by Otto Charles.[98]

Chaffee and Moffat also divided responsibilities successfully. Chaffee often relied on Eben Smith to examine and manage his many mining enterprises.[99] However, according to a contemporary Colorado businessman, Chaffee was sufficiently knowledgeable of mining to profitably advise Moffat, his investment partner and the president of the First National Bank of Denver:

> Chaffee paid more attention to mining matters than Moffat did because that had been his business since 1860. He devoted himself entirely to mining matters and it was through Chaffee largely, that Moffat went into mining. . . . In regard to the reciprocal relationship between Moffat and Chaffee I guess it was about an equal thing.
> Chaffee knew more about mining and Moffat paid more attention to the bank and they were partners in the two concerns.[100]

Mining technicians and financiers found that a division of labor and mutual trust promoted successful partnerships. Whether the western mining entrepreneur was primarily a financier or a formally trained or practical technician, he was usually forced to acquire more capital and technical expertise than he alone could command. Contrary to some popular assumptions, he was neither a rugged individualist or a jack-of-all-trades. The size and complexity of his properties required cooperation and teamwork rather than individualism and self-reliance.

Capital was secured through the combined efforts of partners, bankers, stockholders, and stockbrokers who were willing either to pool their resources, pay assessments, advance loans, or promote and market corporate securities. As examiners and promoters of mining properties, public and private technicians also were an indispensable part of the entrepreneur's fund-raising team. However, government technicians were likely to criticize the capitalist if he arranged with professional promoters and financiers to exploit his mine excessively or manipulate its stock. The uneasy alliance between capital and technology sometimes helped to produce significant, short-term speculative profits, but long-range success was also fostered by a more harmonious union.

Most bonanza kings realized that it was more profitable, in the long run, to learn from technicians and scientists than to exploit or to abuse them. As mining became more technologically demanding, carefully selected technicians were relied upon to provide the necessary advice and managerial skill. As government employees, members of professional organizations, superintendents, consulting engineers, inventors, and managing partners, they formed complementary alliances with the owners of mining properties, and thus helped ensure long-term developmental profit.

Seven

MINING AS BIG BUSINESS

By the 1890s, mining had become big business. Success in the industry demanded the organization and coordination of many supporting facilities and materials. Mining properties required sampling and assaying works, mills, smelters, and refineries to reduce the crude ore. In turn, these reduction plants depended upon the mines to deliver consistently the appropriate type, grade, and amount of ore. Mining or reduction properties also required water, lumber, coal, machinery, and other materials. However, the necessary materials and facilities were expensive and sometimes inaccessible unless a cheap, rapid form of transportation connected the suppliers and the buyers. Railroads thus became the lifeline of the industry, delivering raw materials, ore, and bullion and making it possible to reduce low-grade ore profitably. The bonanza kings established railroads and suppliers of such principal resources as water, lumber, and coal as independent companies or as integral parts of their mining and reduction companies. Mines, sampling and assaying works, mills, smelters, and refineries also were organized separately as independent companies or together in large, diverse corporations. As a result of such organization, entrepreneurs increased efficiency, ensured continuous production, and sometimes defrauded the investing public.

Water has always been especially crucial to the success of business in the trans-Mississippi West. It was a prerequisite for the development of the cattle, farming, and mining industries. As they expanded, their need for water grew, straining the area's limited resources. Although competition for water was intense in the West, mining enterprises generally were located close enough to natural supplies to escape the problems of the Great Plains. Much of the Great Plains is semiarid, receiving less than twenty inches of rainfall annually. Minimal precipitation and the persistent threat of drought forced cattle barons and farmers to adopt water laws and farming methods which conserved the available resources. Mining, on the other hand, developed in the mountains where lakes, reservoirs, streams, and springs usually provided a sufficient supply.

Water was used extensively in hydraulic mining. Entire hillsides of gold-bearing gravel were washed away by powerful jets of water, and the precious metal was collected in sluices. Water power also operated stamp mills. Rushing streams and rivers propelled waterwheels and enabled the stamps to crush the raw ore. Sluices of water conveyed pulverized ore from the batteries in which it was crushed to settling tanks. From there the ore was placed in amalgamating pans where water was added to thin it to the consistency required for grinding.[1]

When converted into steam, water performed other functions. In particular, it heated the pans and the retorts and thereby facilitated the amalgamation and separation of gold and mercury. It also provided the power to operate the mills and smelters and the hoisting, pumping, and drilling machinery used in the mines. Before the introduction of hydroelectric power in the late 1880s and 1890s, these facilities depended almost exclusively on the steam boiler and engine.

The bonanza kings were forced to go to great pains and expense to obtain water. In order to supply his mills in Nevada's Cortes mining district, Simeon Wenban erected a network of pipes and drilled two artesian wells at a cost of $60,000. Bela Buell faced a serious problem near Central City, Colorado. He had access to 22,000 gallons of water but 200,000 gallons were needed daily to operate his properties. The same water had to be used repeatedly. Therefore, he built a series of settling tanks with a total capacity of 500,000 gallons to cleanse the water for reuse in the mill. The tanks were constructed with two-inch planks and had double walls with manure packed between them which made the tanks watertight and frost resistant. Alvinza Hayward relied upon a system of canals and reservoirs to provide his Plymouth Consolidated Gold Mining Company in California with sufficient water. In 1885, it cost him nearly $9,000 to operate these facilities.[2]

Sometimes construction and operating costs were increased by court fights over the title to water supplies. The Homestake Mining Company and its major rival, the Father DeSmet mine, waged a legal and political battle for some time before the former won control of Boulder Ditch and thus a near monopoly over the water from Whitewood Creek, the major supply in the region. Eventually the Homestake acquired nearly all the water rights in the northern Black Hills, "a key factor in the dominance" of the company.[3] Litigation also threatened Jesse Knight. In 1909, he was accused of illegally using Swassie Springs in Millard County, Utah, for his mining and milling operations. The injured party claimed a prior right:

> I hereby notify you and the Ibex Gold Mining Company to repair the damage that your employees have done to the property of my associates and myself. We have a perfected right through the State Engineer's Office to the waters of the spring for a certain period in the year . . . and have, at considerable expense secured a perfect title to water there. We trust that you will treat us fairly in this matter and not force us into a law suit with such a powerful corporation.[4]

The title to water resources sometimes was as difficult to secure as was the title to claims and mines, thereby increasing the total cost of delivery systems. To cover the cost, bonanza kings at times formed water corporations. Among these was the Virginia and Gold Hill Water Company, capitalized at $250,000 by the members of the San Francisco "bank crowd" in 1862. The corporation bought or leased streams near the Comstock Lode and conducted the water through flumes and ditches into large cisterns. Then it was distributed to Virginia City and Gold Hill for domestic and industrial use. Stamp mills and other large consumers monthly payment was $100 per flowing inch. In 1871, John Mackay, James Fair, James Flood, and William O'Brien incorporated a second Virginia and Gold Hill Water Company and purchased all the rights and franchises of the original organization. Water was conducted about twenty miles from sources in the Sierra Nevada to the mines through a network of flumes, dams, reservoirs, and pipes. The cost of construction and litigation was over two million dollars. The mine works consumed two-thirds of the water, or about 2,800,000 gallons daily.[5] As trustees of major Comstock mining corporations, Mackay, Fair, Flood, and O'Brien awarded advantageous contracts to their own water company. According to a contemporary report in the *San Francisco Chronicle*, "duty required them to buy as little water as possible and to buy it in the cheapest market; interest dictated they should sell as much as they could, and that in the dearest market."[6] Many small stockholders of the mining corporations were deceived and assessed by the profiteering water company owners.

Thus, bonanza kings secured water by building delivery systems which were organized as independent companies or as integral parts of mining or milling companies. Organization produced an assured source of supply and, in some cases, the opportunity to exploit the mining investor.

Mining properties consumed trees more voraciously than they consumed water. Firewood was used extensively to heat the steam boilers. By 1880, the mine hoisting works and mills on the Comstock had devoured more than two million cords of wood for fuel.[7] Lumber was needed to construct and repair such surface buildings as ore sheds, mill houses, and hoisting works. Large timbers especially were required for underground excavation. As of 1880, six hundred million feet of timber had been buried in the Comstock mines. According to Eliot Lord, this amount could have erected "nearly 30 thousand two-story frame houses (each 40 by 25 feet and containing six rooms) which would comfortably shelter 150,000 inhabitants."[8]

The nearby insatiable demand required the formation of supply companies. The Pacific Wood, Lumber, and Flume Company was organized and owned by Mackay, Fair, Flood, and O'Brien. The company owned the rights to 12,000 acres of dense pine forest near Lake Tahoe in the Sierra Nevada. In the mid-1870s, it was estimated that the tract contained 500,000 cords of wood, 100,000 feet of sawlogs, and 30,000,000 feet of hewn timber. Such companies as the Pacific Wood, Lumber, and Flume Company also were equipped with sawmills. William Clark's Western Montana Lumber Company owned a large mill near Missoula as well as thousands of acres of timberland. Marcus Daly's holdings were more extensive. His Bitter Root Development Company owned vast timber stands and a sawmill in western Montana. When these resources failed to supply adequately his mines and smelters, he negotiated with the Northern Pacific Railroad for additional property. By 1898, he had purchased 700,000 acres of timberland with an estimated stand of over 200,000 feet per acre.[9]

The entrepreneur's right to timber was not secured easily. Litigation plagued timber and water users alike. Apparently Daly was prosecuted for the illegal cutting of timber. Although subsequently dismissed, suits were brought against N. P. Hill for cutting timber on government lands in Gilpin County, Colorado.[10] Reacting to the efforts of the General Land Office to restrict exploitation of the public domain in Montana, Samuel Hauser complained, "If we are not allowed to cut timber on public lands, it will stop all mining and set the Territory back ten years there being no way to secure title to the land."[11]

Despite legal problems, lumber companies flourished. Although some bonanza kings contracted with independent loggers and woodcutters, many evidently found that their own companies assured supplies at less expense. Others realized that their lumber companies, like their water companies, could be used to exploit the mining investor. The *San Francisco Chronicle* criticized Mackay, Fair, Flood, and O'Brien for awarding very generous contracts to lumber companies they controlled at the expense of stockholders in mining corporations.[12]

Lumber companies could not satisfy the fuel needs of reduction properties. Smelters and refineries required a hotter, more efficient blast for their furnaces than wood or charcoal provided. Therefore, entrepreneurs extended their operations into the coal fields. In 1886, Hauser organized the Livingston Coke and Coal Company to supply his Wickes, Montana, smelter and to overcome the excessive cost of importing coal from Pennsylvania or abroad. The company, which was capitalized at $250,000, leased and purchased properties near Bozeman, Montana. It never produced profitably for an independent market, but it lowered the price of coke for the Wickes smelter from over twenty dollars to $11.50 per ton.[13]

Coal companies were owned or controlled by other bonanza kings. Matthew Walker of the Walker Brothers was a director and major stockholder of Utah's Independent Coal and Coke Company. Horace Tabor organized the Leadville Smelters Supply Company, which furnished his mining and smelting properties with coke, charcoal, and other supplies.[14] Perhaps Jerome Wheeler was the most successful producer and distributor of coal products. In the early 1880s, his Aspen smelter was one hundred miles from the nearest source of coal. The nearly prohibitive cost of transportation forced him to look elsewhere. At Jerome Park, thirty-five miles from Aspen, he purchased coal fields and erected ovens which supplied his smelting works continuously with excellent coke. According to a contemporary reporter, "this investment insured the success of the Aspen Smelting Company."[15] It also encouraged Wheeler to organize the Grand River Coal and Coke Company in 1886. During the 1890s, the company owned and controlled 5,000 acres of coal lands. Its ovens daily produced 2,000 tons of coking, domestic, and steam coal which was sold as far east as the Missouri River.[16] Supply companies sometimes became independently profitable, finding markets beyond their owners' mines, mills, or smelters.

Mining properties also had to be supplied with crushing, hoisting, drilling, and pumping equipment. Iron foundries and machine shops were established in San Francisco as early as 1849. By 1868, fifteen were serving California, Nevada, and other western mining regions. Although most bonanza kings contracted with independent manufacturers, some produced their own equipment. H. R. Wolcott of the Boston and Colorado Smelting Company was the president of Denver's Hendey and Meyer Engineering Company, incorporated in 1884 to manufacture steam engines and other mining, milling, and smelting machinery. Lloyd Tevis was a large stockholder in the Risdon Iron Works of San Francisco. Knight's Supply Company furnished his mines and reduction works with mechanical tools and railroad track. Andrew Jackson Davis owned and operated foundries in

Helena and Butte. During the agricultural depression of the early 1870s, he purchased twenty-seven flour mills and converted them into mining machinery. In 1876, he supplied his own mine, the Lexington, and other Butte properties with stamp mills worth $80,000. In association with Hauser, Davis became one of the leading importers and manufacturers of mining machinery in Montana Territory.[17]

Bonanza kings found the ownership of raw materials and supply companies profitable. Control of such primary materials as water, lumber, coal, and machinery and a host of such secondary ones as powder, limestone, and wire encouraged economical, uninterrupted production. Specifically, the ownership of supply companies eliminated the fear of having to pay an outsider excessive prices for limited natural resources and gave entrepreneurs the opportunity to line their own pockets at the mining stockholder's expense. Some supply companies became self-supporting, serving properties other than their owners' mines and reduction plants. However, service sometimes was slow and expensive.

When mining districts were initially organized, property holders relied upon toll roads and mule-drawn wagons for access to markets and supplies. However, winter snows and spring floods frequently made the roads impassable, forcing mills and mines to stop production. In 1885, David Moffat's Leadville manager complained, "Little ore shipped while absent owing to bad roads and want of hauling facilities, horses having the foot rot which is common here in muddy times."[18] On February 1, 1888, Simeon Reed's superintendent, Victor Clement, also filed a discouraging report: "Hauling this month will be expensive, owing to the frozen and broken up condition of roads on the hill—I am running now partly by sleighs and partly by wagons."[19] In particular, low-grade ores were affected adversely by poor road conditions. They could not be reduced profitably because of the cost of transportation. In 1871, it was reported that more than one million tons of low-grade ore from Arizona's Vulture mine was dumped.[20] It became increasingly apparent that railroads were needed to provide cheaper, faster, more reliable service.

Public officials and private investors recognized the necessity. After surveying the mining regions of the Far West in 1871, Lieutenant George M. Wheeler of the U.S. Army Corps of Engineers recommended the construction of narrow-gauge railroads.[21] Entrepreneurs were reluctant to invest in mining properties unless railroads were available or feasible. In 1908, Knight informed an Arizona mine owner, "The distance your property is from [the] railway may determine largely as to whether I shall care to look into its merits."[22]

The bonanza kings often promoted or constructed railroads to serve their properties. During the late 1880s, Joseph DeLamar became a director of the Idaho North and South Railroad Company and surveyed a prospective route designed to connect his mines and mills at De-Lamar, Idaho, with the Oregon Short Line at Caldwell, Idaho. However, he sold his properties before the road was completed. Most entrepreneurs continued operations long enough to reap the benefits of improved transportation. In 1869, William Sharon and the other members of the Union Mill and Mining Company constructed the Virginia and Truckee Railroad from Virginia City to the company's mills near Carson City. Ormsby and Storey Counties, the mining companies dependent upon the Bank of California, and the bank itself financed the twenty-one-mile road at a cost of $1,750,000. By 1872, the railroad had been extended from Carson City to Reno, where it met the Central

Pacific.[23] According to Eliot Lord, transportation costs had been reduced significantly even before the extension was completed:

> The price of cord-wood delivered in Virginia City . . . fell from $15 to $11.50, and contracts were offered for delivery in the spring of 1870 at $9 per cord. Two dollars per ton was charged for carrying ore from the mines to the Carson River Mills instead of $3.50 per ton, as previously, and the cost of transporting other articles was proportionally diminished. A natural result of this reduction was to bring into market a large amount of ore lying on the mine-dumps or still left in the lode as too poor to pay the charges for transportation and milling. The first ore shipped over the railroad was 7 car-loads, 60 tons in all, from the 700-foot level of the Yellow Jacket Mine, of a grade which had been considered too poor to reduce and had been used as waste rock to fill abandoned drifts.[24]

Clark also profited by substituting railroads for wagon roads. When he purchased the United Verde Copper Company in the late 1880s, only a wagon road sixty miles long connected the United Verde mine near Jerome, Arizona, with the nearest railroad depot, Ash Fork on the Santa Fe. In 1894, he constructed a narrow-gauge road approximately twenty-six miles from Jerome to Phoenix, where it intersected a recently completed branch of the Santa Fe. The intersection was called Jerome Junction, and the company-owned line was named the United Verde and Pacific Railway. Regarded as "the crookest line in the world," this unique road lowered previous transportation costs and made it possible to develop the mine profitably.[25]

Wheeler realized that the development of his Aspen properties depended upon improved transportation. Mule and wagon trains charged exorbitant rates to deliver ore to the Leadville smelters and to return with fuel and mining equipment. As the vice-president and a major stockholder of the Colorado Midland Railroad Company, he decided to extend the road from Leadville to Aspen. The route presented serious engineering problems, and the road was not completed until 1888, a year after the rival Denver and Rio Grande Railroad reached Aspen. The camp's boom period began with the arrival of the railroads. The value of ore produced in Pitkin County from 1888 to 1893 increased more than tenfold over the previous five-year period. The Colorado Midland later was extended to New Castle, where Wheeler owned coal fields. The railroad linked his mining, smelting, and supply operations and helped to ensure continuous production at reasonable costs.[26]

Moffat was more active in building railroads than was Wheeler. During the late 1860s, he was largely responsible for connecting Denver with the transcontinental Union Pacific–Central Pacific. Hoping to make Denver the hub of a vast railroad network, he began construction of a direct line through the Rockies from Denver to Salt Lake City. The line was completed after his death. While the president of the Denver and Rio Grande Railroad Company, 1884–91, he built branch lines to Colorado's major mining camps, where his investments usually were extensive. To overcome expensive and inadequate wagon transportation, he constructed a railroad from Florence on the Denver and Rio Grande system to Cripple Creek, where he and Eben Smith owned the Victor, Golden Cycle, and Anaconda mines. The Florence and Cripple Creek became a small railroad system with branch lines to all the large mines in the district.[27] This railroad and others owned or controlled by Moffat fostered efficient operations at his mines and smelters.

In some respects Hauser was Moffat's Montana counterpart. As the primary Montana representative of the Northern Pacific Railroad, 1880–93, he promoted and constructed branch lines to districts where he held mining properties. After becoming president of the Helena Mining and Reduction Company, he arranged with the Northern Pacific to build a line from Helena to Wickes, where his smelter was located. By late 1883, the Helena and Jefferson County Railroad had been completed, lowering freight rates on raw ore and making it possible to ship bullion east for $35.00 per ton less than previously. In 1887, Hauser also presided over the company which built a railroad from Missoula to the Bitter Root Valley, where he owned silver property. From 1883 to 1890, he was responsible for the construction of at least nine of the Northern Pacific's branch lines. Sizable profits were made when the railroad companies were bonded for a higher sum than the total cost of construction. Hauser's privileged position and competition from the Montana Central and the Union Pacific encouraged the Northern Pacific to grant rebates. He retained a rebate ranging from $1.00 to $2.50 per ton on concentrates and ores sent from his Idaho properties and on bullion shipped eastward by the Wickes smelter.[28]

Other mining entrepreneurs were not as fortunate as Hauser. During the 1880s, the Northern Pacific monopolized the traffic in the Coeur d'Alene mining district. Reed and other mine owners who shipped ore east to Wickes for smelting were forced to pay high freight rates.[29] In 1888, Reed, apparently hoping to reduce transportation costs, tried unsuccessfully to induce an eastern investor to build a smelter and refinery at Portland:

> The great advantage Portland has over, Salt Lake—Helena—Great Falls, Pueblo—Denver—Omaha and other interior points is in getting its Lead product to New York for a Market—Many of these interior points are tied up to one Railroad which can dictate terms, while in that respect Portland now has, the "Northern Pacific"—"Union Pacific" "Southern Pacific" and "Canadian Pacific" and several others pointing this way . . . I have no doubt that Lead could be shipped from Portland to New York at a less price by Rail, than from Salt Lake or Montana points.[30]

Reed's argument revealed the advantages of competing railroads.

Some bonanza kings built competing lines in order to overcome monopoly rates. In 1899, Irving Howbert became the president of the Colorado Springs and Cripple Creek District Railway Company. The company was organized by Howbert and other Springs residents who owned Cripple Creek mines and wanted to build reduction mills in Colorado Springs to compete with those at Florence and Pueblo. Excessive transportation costs charged by the Florence and Cripple Creek Railroad made it uneconomical to reduce the ore in Colorado Springs until the competing road, the Cripple Creek Short Line, was completed in 1902.[31] According to Howbert, "it had not been in operation any great length of time until the construction of additional reduction works in the vicinity of Colorado Springs was under way. . . . Within three or four years from the time the new road began operations, a large part of all Cripple Creek ores was being treated in reduction works adjacent to Colorado Springs."[32]

Thus, many mining entrepreneurs owned, controlled, or otherwise were interested in railroads. They increased production by making it possible to process low-grade ore. Production costs decreased because at times rebates were granted to mining or smelting entrepreneurs who held railroad stock or offices. Improved transportation systems helped ensure continuous, inexpensive operations.

The bonanza kings also sought to reduce transportation expenses by locating reduction plants close to railroad terminals and sources of supplies. Clark realized the advantage of a central location. In 1912, he moved his old Jerome smelter to a site that offered adequate water, a large deposit of clay for building brick, sufficient sand and gravel for construction purposes, a satisfactory area for the disposal of slag and tailings, easy access to the Santa Fe Railroad, and a townsite suitable for ex-

pansion. Hill and James Grant also moved their reduction plants to better, more centrally located areas. In
1878, Hill transferred his smelter from Blackhawk to
Argo, near Denver. In 1882, Grant erected a new smelter
in Denver after fire destroyed his Leadville plant. The
new locations had the advantage of being nearer raw
materials such as coal, a larger labor force, and better
railroad connections.[33]

Entrepreneurs were interested in building reduction
plants close enough to their mines to permit tramway
service. In 1874, Buell lowered his hauling costs significantly by using a tramway rather than mule-drawn
wagons to deliver ore from the Leavitt mine to his
nearby stamp mill. Wheeler installed an electric tramway to carry ore from his mine to his mill in Aspen,
Colorado. Thomas Walsh also relied on the fast, efficient
service of a two-mile-long electric tramway at his Camp
Bird properties.[34]

Magnates used the tramway to supplement rather
than to replace the railroad. Thomas Kearns depended
on a huge aerial tramway, 7,300 feet long, consisting of
eighty buckets and thirty-nine steel towers, to transport
the silver-lead concentrates from his Silver King mine to
the railroad loading station at Park City, Utah. According to Kearns's biographer, "it was a tremendous operation and spelled the success of the Silver King."[35] In the
1890s, Moffat connected the ore house of his Amethyst
mine in Creede with the Denver and Rio Grande by a
tramway which carried 250 tons of ore daily. He also
invested in the Denver Tramway Company.[36] However,
the strategic location of reduction plants perhaps was as
important for success as the control or ownership of railroad and tramway facilities.

Successful gold- and silver-mine owners frequently operated such reduction plants as their own stamp mills.
Rather than trusting independent mills which crushed

ore for a fee, mine owners constructed plants especially
designed to process their particular type and grade of ore
economically. Since they mined on a large scale, the
entrepreneurs usually had sufficient ore to warrant
operating their own mills. Mines and mills at times were
organized together in one company. Reed's Conner Creek
Mining and Milling Company and the Homestake Mining Company are examples of collective organization.

Mines controlled and mills owned by the same entrepreneurs also were organized separately. The advantages were realized by Mackay, Fair, Flood, and O'Brien,
who owned the Pacific Mill and Mining Company and
controlled the Consolidated Virginia and the California
Mining Companies. Just as they had done with their
water and lumber companies, so the partners made
advantageous contracts with themselves:

> As trustees of the Consolidated Virginia . . . it was their duty to
> get the ores of the Company milled as cheaply as possible, and to
> obtain the highest possible percentage of the metals from them. As
> Directors of the Pacific Mill Company, and owning all the stock in
> the Company, it was their interest to mix high-grade ore with
> low-grade ore or with country rock, so that they might mill as
> many tons as possible at the highest rates they could extort, and to
> return as low a percentage as possible to the Consolidated Virginia
> Mining Company, so that the slimes and tailings which they were
> to retain might be the more enriched.[37]

The practice was not unique to the so-called bonanza
firm. William Ralston and Sharon also cheated the stockholders of the mines. The ore from mines which they
controlled was processed by their own organization, the
Union Mill and Mining Company, on very favorable
terms. It was customary for Comstock mills to pay the
mines 65 percent of the value of their ore as determined
periodically by assays of samples. If a higher percentage
was recovered, it was to go to the mine owner. However,
according to Rodman Paul, "the mill operators found it to

their interest to pay only the 65 percent plus enough more of any excess to make the mill look efficient. A surplus beyond that became a hidden extra margin of profit, which went to the 'inside' few."[38] As owners of milling companies and officials of mining companies, entrepreneurs profited from efficiency and unscrupulousness.

Bonanza kings who owned or controlled ore-sampling and assaying works were in a position to cheat their suppliers. During the 1890s, some leading Cripple Creek mining entrepreneurs were "financing crooked assayers and crooked sampling firms."[39] The latter bought ore from small mine owners unable to afford the cost of reduction. The price paid was determined by assaying samples. Winfield Stratton's extensive interests in the Omaha and Grant Smelting Company and in two ore-sampling firms at Victor and Cripple Creek make his operations somewhat suspect. Whether used for legitimate or illegitimate purposes, sampling and assaying works apparently were profitable. In 1880, Grant united his smelting business with Leadville's Eddy and James Sampling Works. Knight owned the Utah Ore Sampling Company, which operated facilities at Murray, Silver City, Sandy, and Park City, Utah. These plants appraised ore from his properties such as the Beck Tunnel and Ibex mines before it was reduced independently or at his Tintic smelter.[40] The ownership of sampling companies protected mining entrepreneurs from unscrupulous middlemen and also afforded the opportunity to cheat ore suppliers by fraudulent assays.

Smelting companies sometimes created problems for mining entrepreneurs. In the late 1880s, Reed faced an apparent conspiracy between the Northern Pacific Railroad and Hauser's Helena Mining and Reduction Company to keep the cost of transportation and smelting high.[41] Reed's superintendent outspokenly opposed such tactics:

The excessive charges for freights and ore-smelting is ruinous to profitable investments. . . . It amounts to exhausting the mines for the benefit of others—It requires a remarkably good mine to stand this strain long. As a general proposition, a mine is worked cheapest at the first stage of its existence—expenses multiplying as depth, water etc are encountered. . . . If the margin for profit is not a good one to start with, the result is clear, that a mine will cease to be profitable at an early period. I have no doubt that R.R. Co's and smelters are aware of this, and will lower their rates accordingly, otherwise they would be cutting off their own noses. The natural induction from this state of things, is, whether it is policy for mine owners to submit to this exaction, for it is equivalent to precipitating their own destruction. The R.R. Co's and Smelters' policy is of a sliding scale nature—they will raise on charges as miners improve on their immediate profits, or lower as they approach the boundary where it ceases to be profitable. The only way practically speaking to meet the difficulty, is for miners to act in concert.[42]

In 1889, Reed, hoping to reduce his smelting expenses and to enhance the resale value of his properties, took an option on the Selby Smelting and Lead Company of San Francisco.[43] However, for some unknown reason he never purchased the company. In 1890, his problems were complicated by the formation of the United Smelting and Refining Company. He wrote to his manager, "I see by this morning's Oregonian a telegram dated Chicago Mar 2d stating that nearly all the Smelters have combined in a trust with Capital of $25,000,000 to stand off the 'Lead Trust.' It will next be in order for the Mines to combine."[44] Unable to rely on competition to reduce the cost of ore reduction, Reed's successors at the Bunker Hill and Sullivan bought control of a Tacoma smelter and later, in 1917, built their own smelter at Kellogg near the mines.[45]

Many bonanza kings avoided Reed's problems. Daly, Hauser, Moffat, Wheeler, Clark, and others operated their own smelters. In 1889, Clark was instrumental in establishing the Colorado and Montana Smelting Com-

pany, which built Butte's first smelter and thereby
eliminated the expense of transporting ore to distant
Colorado reduction plants. By purchasing the ores of
various mines, Clark was able to obtain the proper fluxing mixture for the efficient and successful operation of
the smelter.[46]

Fluxing ores were a major part of the smelting process,
but they were not always secured easily. Knight's Tintic
Smelting Company failed after one year in part because
the expense of transporting these ores was nearly prohibitive. In order to run efficiently and at full capacity,
smelters required an abundant and carefully selected ore
supply. Therefore, such smelting entrepreneurs as Hauser, Grant, and Wolcott acquired ore not only from their
own mines but also from independent producers and
sampling companies.[47] Walsh had trouble obtaining the
kind of ore necessary for the most efficient smelting
charge. In 1894, he wrote to his partner about the prospects of their Silverton Smelting and Mining Company:

> We have had an awful time for silicious ores. We have had none to
> speak of from the start. Owners of those ores here have been trying
> to make us pay them their prices and we have been boycotted to
> some extent—We have had no supply of quartz from the first. It
> was only by using old dumps often-times at a ruinous treatment
> charge that we were able to keep running or to make a run of any
> duration, and then we had to run from the hand to the mouth,
> sampling small lots, charges daily, which latter is very hurtful to a
> furnace. . . . I have been in hopes from time to time that we could
> improve the silicious ore market, but it is as bad today as it has
> been, and unless a good mine can be acquired by either the com-
> pany or its friends I dont see how we can fix it. . . . There are
> millions of tons in the camp but they are not able to stand a high
> treatment [cost]. The purchase of a few mines here near town
> would make the company perfectly independent in this respect. . . .
> If the Lord will carry me through this one [venture] I certainly will
> never have anything to do with another unless there is an
> abundant capital as well as an abundance of all kinds of ores
> before starting.[48]

Thus, by operating their own reduction facilities relatively close to their mines, entrepreneurs avoided the excessive fees of outside smelters and expensive railroad rates. They also found that the ownership of carefully selected mines helped assure an abundant supply of appropriate ores for their smelters.

Refining, which completed the reduction of complex ores, was often done in the East or sometimes abroad by companies not owned or controlled by the bonanza kings. For a variety of reasons refining was uneconomical in Montana. Therefore, Hauser initially shipped the base bullion from his Helena Mining and Reduction Company to the Newark Smelting and Refining Works in New Jersey. After 1885, his buyers included the Chicago Smelting and Refining Company and the Pennsylvania Lead Company of Pittsburgh. However, some entrepreneurs who did extensive smelting found that they could also refine their ore economically. Dennis Sheedy combined both operations in his Globe Smelting and Refining Company. After Thomas Selby's death in 1875, the Selby Smelting and Lead Company of San Francisco purchased the property of the Pacific Refinery and Bullion Exchange. As of 1889, the Selby firm was the only smelting, refining, and manufacturing company of its kind on the Pacific Coast. In 1873, Hill's Boston and Colorado Smelting Company added a refinery, thereby eliminating the expense of having its copper matte refined in Swansea, Wales.[49] In 1882, Grant united his Denver smelter with a refinery in Omaha, creating the Omaha and Grant Smelting Company, then "one of the greatest industrial institutions that has . . . been founded at any point between the Missouri River and San Francisco."[50] The quantity and variety of ores smelted by Grant and others justified the ownership of refineries.

Sometimes the bonanza kings included the manufacture and sale of metal and mineral products among their many operations. The Selby Smelting and Lead Company produced lead pipe, sheet lead, bar lead, pig lead, lead traps, antifriction metal, block tin pipes, and machine-loaded shotgun cartridges. Wheeler owned a plant which manufactured mineral paints and glass at Colorado City. Clark took advantage of the increasing use of electricity after 1890 by establishing a wireworks in Elizabethport, New Jersey, which produced one hundred tons of wire every twenty-four hours and became an excellent outlet for his copper mines. The bonanza kings who mined and reduced the ore and manufactured metal or mineral products were not only responding to economic incentives. Some evidently liked the power and prestige of personally and absolutely controlling the various stages of mineral production. Clark, for example, was the president, the board of directors, and the holder of all the stock of fourteen immense corporations.[51] It is unlikely that he would have surrendered the final stage in metal production to a company he did not control.

Some bonanza kings undoubtedly liked to think of themselves as empire builders. That notion might have influenced the organization and expansion of their enterprises, but business decisions were determined primarily by practical considerations. Profits increased when mining entrepreneurs awarded their collateral business on highly favorable terms to their own water, lumber, sampling, or milling companies. Officials of the Union Pacific Railroad Company followed a similar practice when they contracted with the Credit Mobilier Company to construct the railroad for an excessive price. The organization and ownership of related companies was not always motivated by the desire for fraudulent profits. Many bonanza kings improved the efficiency and stability of their operations by owning or controlling strategically located reduction facilities and supply and railroad companies. Others found that business expansion was necessary to ensure a competitive advantage in an industry affected by a steady decline in the price of silver after the mid-1880s and by fluctuations in the price of lead.

Sometimes bonanza kings owned multifunction organizations rather than several interdependent, single-function corporations. The Homestake Mining Company is a good example. It systematically performed all the processes necessary to mining and milling. For example, the company generated its own electricity, repaired its own engines, logged and milled its own timber, sharpened its own drill steel, and forged its own castings. The company's near monolithic structure and constant research and experimentation kept the mine in profitable operation long after allegedly richer mines were exhausted.[52] The Tabor Mines and Mills Company, capitalized at five million dollars in 1892, is another example of business consolidation. The articles of incorporation explain the many functions of this vertically integrated corporation which proposed to own or operate everything that it needed:

> The objects for which our said Company is formed and incorporated are to purchase, locate, lease or otherwise acquire mines, minerals. . . . to carry on the business of mining, milling, quarrying, metallurgical manufacturing, building and other operations . . . to construct, operate, maintain or improve roads, tramways, flumes, ditches, canals, crushing, stamping, amalgamating and other mills buildings, plant apparatus, and works which may be necessary or convenient for the purposes of the company; to reduce, make merchantable, transport and sell, lease, let or otherwise dispose of or deal in the property of the company.[53]

Vertical integration allowed the bonanza kings to control and coordinate efficiently the various phases of production and distribution and specifically provided an assurance of raw materials at satisfactory prices. Similar

motives prompted the expansion of such combines as
Standard Oil and the Carnegie Steel Company. In the
1870s, almost all American industrial companies only
manufactured goods and relied upon commissioned
agents, wholesalers, and other middlemen to provide
their supplies and to sell their finished products. Mining
enterprises behaved in a comparable fashion. By the end
of the century, however, many American industries had
become dominated by a few great companies that not
only manufactured goods, but also sold them directly to
retailers or even to the ultimate consumer and bought or
produced their own basic materials and other supplies.[54]

Some entrepreneurs used the holding company as a
legal device to manage the companies they owned or
controlled. In 1906, the Knight Investment Company
was organized as a holding company for Knight's many
diverse operations. Eventually it controlled eighty corporations, including smelting, mining, railroad, sampling, and electric power companies. Members of the
Knight family served as the board of directors and held
the stock of the various corporations either personally or
as officials of the holding company. For example, in 1910,
nearly 500,000 of the Great Western Gold and Copper
Mining Company's 1,000,000 shares were owned by the
investment company. Jesse Knight personally owned 10
shares and his son, J. William, owned 2,667. The holding
company, like the trust, allowed the bonanza kings to
coordinate the operations of what otherwise were sometimes competing firms. In 1888, competition and rising
production costs forced Hauser to organize the Helena
and Livingston Smelting and Reduction Company as a
holding company for the Helena Mining and Reduction
Company, the Livingston Coke and Coal Company, and
the Gregory Consolidated Mining Company.[55] According
to Hauser's biographer, "the consolidation was one of the
most important to that time in Montana."[56]

By 1900, production costs, competition, and litigation had accelerated consolidation. Heavily capitalized national corporations like the American Smelting and Refining Company, Phelps Dodge, and the Amalgamated Copper Company were beginning to dominate the industry as completely as the bonanza kings had dominated local mining districts and regions. Some entrepreneurs such as Knight, Clark, and Joseph Walker passed control of their companies to their descendants, but many saw their properties absorbed by absentee financiers and by such Standard Oil Company officials as Henry H. Rogers. The bonanza kings were superseded as inexorably as they had replaced the itinerant prospectors. Nonetheless, they contributed the technological knowledge and the managerial and organizational skill upon which their successors constructed the large, decentralized, multidivisional corporations of the twentieth century.

EIGHT

HOW TO SUCCEED IN MINING

THE MINING FRONTIER inevitably brings to mind the stereotype prospector, complete with white beard, red flannels, and the hat turned up characteristically at the brim. This colorful figure has been viewed as an unsophisticated and self-sufficient rugged individualist, subsisting on black coffee and sourdough and tirelessly chasing the rumor and promise of discovery from camp to camp. A pan and a pick were the essential tools of his trade and a mule his only friend. When the "jackass miner" made that lucky strike, he was prepared to defend his claim with a six-shooter or even a lynching party.

The popular conception of success on the mining frontier is more romantic than realistic. Perhaps this fact explains why the irrepressible prospector usually has obscured the contributions of the industrial mining entrepreneur. In this regard the prospector has functioned much as the cowboy. Ray Allen Billington contends that "the true heroes of the Cattle Kingdom were not the cowboys, but the ranchers whose shrewd management allowed the conquest of a new frontier."[1] The same can be said for the mining industrialist, the bonanza king.

Many successful mining industrialists had been prospectors. They had shared the prospector's mobility, optimism, and sometimes even his luck, but these characteristics alone did not make one successful in mining. Good timing was a more important prerequisite. Attracted to the frontier primarily by the promise of instant wealth, future bonanza kings usually joined the early rushes to the major mining regions and districts. An early arrival facilitated the purchase of a productive claim. Mining magnates soon learned to buy property and to expand operations when prices were low and to liquidate their holdings before their value declined. However, success was not simply a matter of buying and selling in the right place at the right time. It required entrepreneurship, or an ability to acquire and to manage property, labor, capital, and technology.

Prospective mining moguls served a long apprenticeship to learn their trade. Independent or formal study of geology, mineralogy, mining engineering, and metallurgy provided technical knowledge. Experience as lode-mine workers, superintendents, merchants, and bankers produced the strategic opportunity or the capital to enter large-scale industrial mining on a profitable basis. However, the examination, purchase, and development of promising properties usually required more expertise and capital than the bonanza king alone possessed. Mining entrepreneurs were forced to rely on partners, stockholders, bankers, stockbrokers, and promoters to help raise the necessary funds. Trained technicians were indispensable as consultants and witnesses in the courtroom and as examiners, promoters, superintendents, and managers of property. Specialization and cooperation were essential to the success of complex, large-scale mining enterprises. The self-sufficiency and individualism of the prospector were of little use.

Nonetheless, not all mining magnates chose cooperation as the most expeditious road to success. Some were exploitative and contentious. They battled their competitors in the mines and in the courtrooms, bribing witnesses, jurors, and even judges to secure the title to property. They used Pinkerton spies, injunctions, military force, lockouts, and blacklists to suppress and to coerce striking workers. They deceived and cheated investors by overcapitalization and by the excessive assessment and manipulation of stock, thereby alienating the government technicians and scientists who objected to such unscrupulous, speculative methods.

Although some bonanza kings adopted the tactics of robber barons in order to succeed, many behaved more like industrial statesmen and pursued a flexible, conciliatory approach to the problems of property, labor, and technology. These entrepreneurs resolved contested ownership by timely agreements compelling the opposing parties to consolidate their holdings under common management. They avoided long, violent strikes by compromise and concession, which helped to produce loyal, efficient workers by placing a higher priority on maximum uninterrupted production than on reduced labor costs. As mining became increasingly sophisticated, they formed productive alliances with technicians and business-minded government scientists who were trained in ore location, extraction, and reduction. In sum, many bonanza kings emphasized long-term, developmental profit over speculative shortcuts and realized that policies which produced cooperation and consensus, rather than just exploitation and conflict, fostered success in the mining industry.

Since Frederick Jackson Turner delivered his famous address, "The Significance of the Frontier in American History," the concept of democracy has frequently been associated with such western pioneers as the miner. In part, Turner defined democracy as the pioneer's "freedom to rise," the result of free land and new economic opportunities. A comparison of the social origins of western mining magnates with those of eastern industrial elites suggests that the frontier provided more vertical social mobility for aspiring businessmen than did the older, more settled areas of the nation. From the standpoint of achieving success in western mining, it was not a disadvantage to have been born poor.

Recent ascent from the lower- or middle-class and experience as working miners perhaps made the bonanza king more responsive to the grievances of labor than his relatively well-born industrial counterpart in the East. Nonetheless, both knew the value of force as well as appeasement. Both increased production by picking talented complementary business associates and by cautiously adopting such technological innovations as the amalgamation and cyanide processes in the mining industry or the Bessemer process and the open-hearth method in the iron and steel industry. Both used interlocking directorships, vertically integrated enterprises, and holding companies to increase efficiency, to ensure continuous production, or to realize fraudulent profits. Together they laid the organizational foundations for the modern industrial corporations of the twentieth century.

Although the bonanza king's business life was not unique, it was diversified. Successful mining entrepreneurs often had been bankers or merchants before entering the industry. Many found banking to be of continued service to their mining interests. Ownership of mining enterprises often led simultaneously to investments in water, lumber, coal, and railroad companies. Some bonanza kings such as Simeon Reed, Marcus Daly, Andrew Davis, and Samuel Hauser bred horses or operated farms or extensive cattle ranches or, like James Haggin and Lloyd Tevis, became active in land reclamation and speculation. Others such as Jesse Knight and William Clark invested in the sugar-beet industry while engaged in mining. Some such as William Ralston, Adolph Sutro, Horace Tabor, and Samuel Newhouse became town planners and builders, investing in hotels, public utilities, real estate, or opera houses in cities like San Francisco,

Denver, and Salt Lake. Several mining magnates, for example Clark, established company towns to accommodate as well as to exploit the needs of their working men. The bonanza kings were as much flexible frontier capitalists as they were mining entrepreneurs. In this sense, they conformed to the jack-of-all-trades stereotype frequently identified with the frontiersman. Their investments contributed not only to the development of the mining frontier but to the growth of the agricultural, ranching, transportation, and urban frontiers. These frontiers did not evolve in the orderly, self-contained, chronological fashion usually suggested by textbooks. They coexisted simultaneously in the business lives of the mining entrepreneurs, who realized that their diverse investments could serve one another. As historians recognize that the economic history of the mining West was neither divorced from the support of surrounding frontiers or from the experiences of businessmen in other parts of the nation, they will appreciate more completely the role of the bonanza kings as an integrating force.

The social life-styles of the bonanza kings further illustrate the connection between the West and the rest of the nation. Many mining magnates indulged in Victorian mansions, exclusive club memberships, the Grand Tour of Europe, lavish parties, patronage of the arts and letters, and large contributions for charity and civic improvement. Some maintained palatial residences in New York City or Washington, D.C., vacationed in fashionable Newport, Rhode Island, and purchased ocean-going yachts, private railroad cars, and racing stables. Apparently the western nouveaux riches were anxious to appear like such famous national industrialists as Cornelius Vanderbilt, John D. Rockefeller, or Andrew Carnegie. Perhaps the West has always felt a sense of cultural inferiority and a need to prove itself by conforming to national standards. The conspicuous consumption and cultural pursuits of eastern elites provided a convenient model, evidently enabling socially ambitious pioneer miners to overcome their provincial doubts and inadequacies. Thus, in their business and social behavior, if not in their social origins, western mining entrepreneurs apparently had more in common with eastern industrialists than with such frontier types as the prospector, popularly known for his unsophistication, individualism, self-sufficiency, and violence.

APPENDIX

Individual	Lifetime	Area
Lemuel S. Bowers	1833–68	California
Charles A. Broadwater	1840–92	Montana
Bela S. Buell	1836–1918	Colorado
Jerome Chaffee	1825–86	Colorado
William A. Clark	1839–1925	Montana, Arizona
Marcus Daly	1841–1900	Montana
Andrew J. Davis	1819–90	Montana
Joseph R. DeLamar	1843–1918	Utah
James G. Fair	1831–94	Nevada
James C. Flood	1826–89	Nevada
John D. Fry	1819–1900	Nevada
James B. Grant	1848–1911	Colorado
James Ben A. Haggin	1822–1914	South Dakota
John H. Hammond	1855–1936	Idaho
A. K. P. Harmon	1821–96	Nevada
Samuel T. Hauser	1833–1914	Idaho, Montana
Alvinza Hayward	1821–1904	California, Nevada
George Hearst	1820–91	South Dakota
F. Augustus Heinze	1869–1914	Montana
Nathaniel P. Hill	1832–1900	Colorado
Irving Howbert	1846–1934	Colorado
John P. Jones	1829–1912	California, Nevada
Thomas Kearns	1862–1918	Utah
David Keith	1847–1918	Utah
Jesse Knight	1845–1921	Utah
John W. Mackay	1831–1902	Nevada
Darius O. Mills	1825–1910	Nevada, Idaho
David H. Moffat	1839–1911	Colorado
Henry Newell	1844–1928	Utah

Individual	Lifetime	Area
Samuel Newhouse	1853–1930	Utah, Colorado
William S. O'Brien	1826–78	Nevada
John Q. Packard	1822–1908	Utah
Almarin B. Paul	1823–1909	California
Thomas C. Power	1839–1923	Montana
William C. Ralston	1826–75	Nevada
Simeon G. Reed	1830–95	Idaho
Thomas Selby	1820–75	California
William Sharon	1821–85	Nevada
Dennis Sheedy	1846–1923	Colorado
Winfield S. Stratton	1848–1902	Colorado
Adolph H. Sutro	1830–98	Nevada
Horace A. Tabor	1830–99	Colorado
Lloyd Tevis	1824–99	South Dakota
Joseph R. Walker	1836–1901	Utah
Matthew H. Walker	1845–1916	Utah
Enos Wall	1839–1920	Utah
Thomas F. Walsh	1851–1910	Colorado
Simeon Wenban	1824–?	Nevada
Jerome B. Wheeler	1841–1918	Colorado
Henry R. Wolcott	1846–1921	Colorado

*Most of these individuals invested in many mining areas throughout the West and even in Latin America. Thus, identification with one or two districts becomes somewhat arbitrary and unrepresentative.

NOTES

Introduction

1. Lewis Atherton, *The Cattle Kings* (Bloomington: Indiana University Press, 1961), p. xi.

2. See Sidney Ratner, ed., *New Light on the History of Great American Fortunes, American Millionaires of 1892 and 1902* (New York: Augustus M. Kelley, Inc., 1953). The 1892 survey listed the occupations in which the fortunes were made.

3. C. Wright Mills, "The American Business Elite: A Collective Portrait," *Journal of Economic History* 5 (special issue *The Tasks of Economic History*) (December 1945): 20.

4. Rodman W. Paul, *Mining Frontiers of the Far West, 1848–1880* (New York: Holt, Rinehart, and Winston, 1963), p. 194.

5. The availability of adequate biographical information in part prompted Frances Gregory and Irene Neu to select their sample of industrial leaders from the decade 1870–79. Frances W. Gregory and Irene D. Neu, "The American Industrial Elite in the 1870s, Their Social Origins," in *Men in Business: Essays in the History of Entrepreneurship*, ed. William Miller (Cambridge, Mass.: Harvard University Press, 1952), p. 195.

Chapter 1

1. Frederick Jackson Turner, *The Frontier in American History* (New York: Henry Holt and Co., 1920), pp. 259, 293. The first part of this quotation appeared originally in a commencement address at the University of Washington on June 17, 1914.

2. William A. Reavis, "The Maryland Gentry and Social Mobility, 1637–1676," *William and Mary Quarterly* 14 (July 1957): 418–28; Kenneth A. Lockridge, *A New England Town, the First Hundred Years: Dedham, Massachusetts, 1636–1736* (New York: W. W. Norton and Co., 1970), pp. 72–74, 141–42, 151–52; Charles S. Grant, *Democracy in the Connecticut Frontier Town of Kent* (New York: Columbia

University Press, 1961), pp. 29–103; Nancy C. Roberson, "Social Mobility in Ante-bellum Alabama," *Alabama Review* 13 (April 1960): 135–45; and Merle Curti, *The Making of an American Community: A Case Study of Democracy in a Frontier County* (Stanford, Calif.: Stanford University Press, 1959), pp. 57–65, 154–62, 187–221, 443–45.

3. Ralph Mann, "The Decade after the Gold Rush: Social Structure in Grass Valley and Nevada City, California, 1850–1860," *Pacific Historical Review* 41 (November 1972): 484–504; William G. Robbins, "Opportunity and Persistence in the Pacific Northwest: A Quantitative Study of Early Roseburg, Oregon," *Pacific Historical Review* 39 (August 1970): 279–96; Peter J. Coleman, "Restless Grant County: Americans on the Move," *Wisconsin Magazine of History* 96 (Autumn 1962): 16–20. Merle Curti also discovered a rapid turnover of population in Trempealeau County, Wisconsin, in the 1860s, and that "somewhat larger percentages of low-property groups than of higher-property groups moved on." However, he explained that "there was great turnover in all age groups, all nativity groups, and all property groups . . . [and that] it cannot be assumed that all or even most of those who left had failed or 'given up,' since moving was the order of the day." (Curti, *Making of an American Community*, pp. 65–77, 257–58, 446). See also George Blackburn and Sherman Richards, Jr., "A Demographic History of the West: Manistee County, Michigan, 1860," *Journal of American History* 57 (December 1970): 600–618. During the eighteenth century, Chester County, Pennsylvania, experienced a redistribution of wealth which favored the upper and upper-middle strata. See James T. Lemon and Gary B. Nash, "The Distribution of Wealth in Eighteenth-Century America: A Century of Change in Chester County, Pennsylvania, 1693–1802," *Journal of Social History* 2 (Fall 1968): 1–24. Economic inequality was not necessarily unique to pioneer counties or western cities. Boston's maritime society became increasingly more stratified and unequal between 1687 and 1771. See James A. Henretta, "Economic Development and Social Structure in Colonial Boston," *William and Mary Quarterly* 22 (January 1965): 75–92.

4. Stephan Thernstrom, *Poverty and Progress: Social Mobility in a Nineteenth Century City* (Cambridge, Mass.: Harvard University Press, 1964), pp. 197–98; and idem, *The Other Bostonians: Poverty and Progress in the American Metropolis, 1880–1970* (Cambridge, Mass.: Harvard University Press, 1973), pp. 241–50.

5. It was not always possible to obtain complete or consistently reliable biographical information even for the limited sample of fifty

individuals used in this study. To ensure accuracy, numerous sources
were used, and the data available in each were checked against those
available in the others. In a few cases (e.g., the attempt to determine
class membership) qualitative rather than quantitative data had to
be relied on. Much space would be required to list all the sources
examined for biographical information. In addition to the various
primary and secondary sources cited in the introduction, suffice to say
that information was provided by such biographical encyclopedias as
Hubert H. Bancroft, *Chronicles of the Builders of the Commonwealth*,
7 vols. (San Francisco: History Co., 1891–1892); William N. Byers,
Encyclopedia of Biography of Colorado (Chicago: Century Publishing
and Engraving Co., 1901); and Myron Angel, *History of Nevada with
Illustrations and Biographical Sketches of Its Prominent Men and
Pioneers* (Berkeley, Calif.: Howell-North, 1958; originally published,
1881). Interviews conducted by Hubert Bancroft's staff proved invaluable for information on mining leaders from California, Nevada,
and Colorado. The California Historical Society and the State Division of Utah History (formerly the Utah State Historical Society)
provided biographical facts on Alvinza Hayward and the Walker
brothers, respectively. *Who Was Who in America*, state and local
histories, and newspaper obituaries were used extensively.

6. William Miller, "American Historians and the Business Elite,"
Journal of Economic History 9 (November 1949): 184–208. Miller
examined 190 presidents and board chairmen of the largest corporations in the following major fields: (1) manufacturing and mining, (2)
steam railroad, (3) public utilities, and (4) finance (commercial banking, life insurance, and investment banking). The companies in
manufacturing and mining, steam railroads, and public utilities were
ranked by capitalization, the commercial banks by deposits, and the
life insurance companies by assets. Also see Gregory and Neu,
"American Industrial Elite," pp. 193–211. The authors chose 303 men
in the top jobs of major companies, which were selected according to
capitalization or production from three prominent industries in the
United States. The top-level occupations were usually those of
president, vice-president, general manager, superintendent, and
treasurer. Of the 303 men, 102 were chosen from textiles (the oldest
large-scale industry in America), 100 from steel (then the newest big
industry), and 101 from railroads. A similar procedure and definition
of entrepreneurial success could have been used exclusively in my
study. However, the results of the criteria used by Miller, Gregory,
and Neu would be distorted in part by watered stock, so common in
the western mining industry, and by inaccurate production reports.

Such criteria also would require the elimination of such prominent individuals as William Ralston of the Bank of California or George Hearst, neither of whom was always the official titular leader of the companies he owned or controlled. There are obvious problems in comparing a sample of 50 men selected throughout the mining West over essentially a thirty-year period with two larger groups of men chosen over two different ten-year periods. However, my comparative findings are meant to be more suggestive than definitive. Further, since relatively few of the general mining population even became notably successful and even fewer were able to sustain their success, I believe that a group of 50 individuals will be fairly representative of western mining elites.

    7. Miller, "American Historians and the Business Elite," p. 200. For the industrial elite of the 1870s, see Gregory and Neu, "American Industrial Elite," p. 197.

    8. Ibid., pp. 197–98. Miller, "American Historians and the Business Elite," p. 201. For Joseph and Matthew Walker, see *Biographical Record of Salt Lake City and Vicinity* (Chicago: National Historical Record Co., 1902), pp. 35–36; Orson F. Whitney, *History of Utah*, 4 vols. (Salt Lake City: George Q. Cannon and Sons, 1892–1904), 4: 626–27; and Henry Hall, ed., *America's Successful Men of Affairs: An Encyclopedia of Contemporaneous Biography*, 2 vols. (New York: New York Tribune, 1895–96), 2: 814–16. For Dennis Sheedy, see Joseph G. McCoy, *History Sketches of the Cattle Trade of the West and Southwest* (Kansas City, Mo.: Ramsey, Millett and Hudson, 1874), pp. 388–89; and Dennis Sheedy, *The Autobiography of Dennis Sheedy* (Denver: Privately printed, 1922), pp. 7–12.

    9. For the problems of Mexicans and other Latin Americans on the California mining frontier, see Richard H. Peterson, *Manifest Destiny in the Mines: A Cultural Interpretation of Anti-Mexican Nativism in California, 1848–1853* (San Francisco: R and E Research Associates, 1975); Leonard Pitt, "The Beginnings of Nativism in California," *Pacific Historical Review* 30 (February 1961): 23–38; and Jay Monaghan, *Chile, Peru, and the California Gold Rush of 1849* (Berkeley: University of California Press, 1973). The Chinese experience is considered by Gunther Barth, *Bitter Strength: A History of the Chinese in the United States, 1850–1870* (Cambridge, Mass.: Harvard University Press, 1964), especially pp. 129–56. Also see Stuart C. Miller, *The Unwelcome Immigrant: The American Image of the Chinese, 1785–1882* (Berkeley: University of California Press, 1969). A brief discussion of French emigrant companies and discrimination against the French in the mines can be found in Abraham P. Nasatir,

The French in the California Gold Rush (New York: American Society of the French Legion of Honor, 1934), pp. 8–11.

10. Gregory and Neu, "American Industrial Elite," p. 199.

11. According to the size of birthplaces for business elites of the 1870s and early twentieth century, a significant majority of leading eastern capitalists were born in the city. See ibid., p. 201; and Miller, "American Historians and the Business Elite," p. 203.

12. William Knight, *The Jesse Knight Family: Jesse Knight, His Forebears and Family* (Salt Lake City: Deseret New Press, 1940), p. 25.

13. In this regard, Miller cites the example of Darwin P. Kingsley, president of the New York Life Insurance Company from 1907 to 1931. He was raised on a forty-acre farm in Vermont. Miller classifies him and others with similar or poorer backgrounds as lower-class in origin (Miller, "American Historians and the Business Elite," pp. 204–5). It was not usually possible to determine the size of the farms on which mining leaders were raised, but every effort to consider all known factors suggests that most of the farmers' sons were raised in circumstances which resembled the boyhood of Jesse Knight or Darwin Kingsley more closely than that of James B. Grant. For James B. Haggin, see Alonzo Phelps, *Contemporary Biography of California's Representative Men,* 2 vols. (San Francisco: A. L. Bancroft and Co., 1881), 1: 325–28.

14. Gregory and Neu, "American Industrial Elite," p. 202.

15. Dwight Akers, "David H. Moffat and His Home Town," *Colorado Magazine* 27 (July 1950): 213–14; Harold A. Boner, *The Giant's Ladder: David H. Moffat and His Railroad* (Milwaukee: Kalmback Publishing Co., 1962), pp. 11–12; and Edgar C. McMechen, *The Moffat Tunnel of Colorado: An Epic of Empire*, 2 vols. (Denver: Wahlgreen Publishing Co., 1927), 1: 44. For Joseph R. DeLamar, see Hall, ed., *America's Successful Men*, 1: 175; and *New York Times*, December 2, 1918. For DeLamar's Idaho career, see G. W. Barrett, "When Big Money Came to Owyhee," *Idaho Yesterdays* 13 (Spring 1969): 2–9, 22–29.

16. Gregory and Neu, "American Industrial Elite," p. 204. William Miller arrives at a similar composite profile for the business elite of the early twentieth century. See Miller, "American Historians and the Business Elite," pp. 207–08.

Chapter 2

1. Augusta Tabor, "Cabin Life in Colorado," MS, 1884, Bancroft Library, University of California, Berkeley, p. 5.

2. Quoted in Robert J. Burdette, ed., *American Biography and Genealogy:* 2 vols. (Chicago: Lewis Publishing Co., 1912), 2: 707. For Jones's early California experiences, see John E. Baur, "Early Days and California Years of John Percival Jones, 1849–1867," *Southern California Quarterly* 44 (June 1962): 97–131.

3. Almarin B. Paul, "My First Two Years in California," *Quarterly of the Society of California Pioneers* 4 (March 1927): 29.

4. John W. Hakola, "Samuel T. Hauser and the Economic Development of Montana: A Case Study in Nineteenth-Century Frontier Capitalism" (Ph.D. diss., Indiana University, 1961), pp. 6–7, 27.

5. Watson Parker, "The Causes of American Gold Rushes," *North Dakota History: Journal of the Northern Plains* 36 (Fall 1969): 343.

6. *Mines and Mining Men of Colorado, Historical, Descriptive and Pictorial: An Account of the Principal Producing Mines of Gold and Silver* (Denver: J. G. Canfield, 1893), pp. 42–43. For a biography of Wheeler, see Bancroft, *Chronicles of the Builders,* 6: 619–43.

7. Sheedy, *Autobiography,* p. 8.

8. Quoted in Thomas F. Dawson, *Life and Character of Edward Oliver Wolcott, Late a Senator of the United States from the State of Colorado,* 2 vols. (New York: Knickerbocker Press, 1911), 1: 80.

9. William Randolph Hearst, Jr., "The Frontier Life—Part 2," *San Francisco Examiner and Chronicle,* August 21, 1966.

10. Quoted in James E. Fell, Jr., "Nathaniel P. Hill, a Scientist-Entrepreneur in Colorado," *Arizona and the West* 15 (Winter 1973): 318.

11. N. P. Hill to wife, June 19, 1864, folio 1, notebook 1, Nathaniel P. Hill Personal Papers, State Historical Society of Colorado, Denver (hereafter cited as Hill Papers).

12. Quoted from an original letter of 1860 by the *Denver Post,* April 21, 1907.

13. For Wall's mining career, see G. W. Barrett, "Colonel E. A. Wall: Mines, Miners, and Mormons," *Idaho Yesterdays* 14 (Fall 1970): 3–11; and Barrett, "Enos Andrew Wall, Mine Superintendent and Inventor," *Idaho Yesterdays* 15 (Spring 1971): 24–31.

14. Quoted in Burdette, *American Biography and Genealogy,* 2:707.

15. Allen Johnson, Dumas Malone, and et al., eds., *Dictionary of American Biography,* 22 vols. and supplements (New York: Charles Scribner's Sons, 1928–58), 13: 6; and Alejandro Perez-Venero, "The 'Forty-Niners through Panama," *Journal of the West* 11 (July, 1972): 460–69.

16. Ethel Manter, *Rocket of the Comstock: The Story of John William Mackay* (Caldwell, Ida.: Caxton Printers, 1950), pp. 55–69;

Oscar Lewis, *Silver Kings: The Lives and Times of Mackay, Fair, Flood, and O'Brien, Lords of the Nevada Comstock Lode* (New York: Alfred A. Knopf, 1967), p. 130; and Paul, *Mining Frontiers*, pp. 40–43.

17. Glenn C. Quiett, *They Built the West: An Epic of Rails and Cities* (New York: Cooper Square Publishers, 1965), p. 166.

18. Horace A. W. Tabor, "Autobiography," MS, 1889, Bancroft Library, University of California, Berkeley, p. 9.

19. Quoted from *Denver Polly Pry*, ca. 1914, newspaper clipping in Thomas F. Dawson, comp., *Scrapbooks*, 80 vols., (Denver, Colo.: State Historical Society of Colorado), 59: 289.

Chapter 3

1. Lewis Atherton, "Structure and Balance in Western Mining History," *Huntington Library Quarterly* 30 (November 1966): 63.

2. The standard biography of Winfield Scott Stratton is Frank J. Waters, *Midas of the Rockies* (Denver: Alan Swallow, 1949). For information about Sandy Bowers, see Angel, *History of Nevada*, p. 622; Wells Drury, *An Editor on the Comstock Lode* (New York: Farrar and Rinehart, 1936), p. 13; and J. Wells Kelly, comp., *First Directory of Nevada Territory, 1862* (Los Gatos, Calif.: Talisman Press, 1962), p. 169. For Jesse Knight, see Gary Fuller Reese, " 'Uncle Jesse,' the Story of Jesse Knight, Miner, Industrialist, Philanthropist" (M.S. thesis, Brigham Young University, 1961), pp. 22–24.

3. McMechen, *The Moffat Tunnel*, 1: 75–76.

4. George T. Marye, Jr., *From '49 to '83 in California and Nevada: Chapters from the Life of George Thomas Marye, a Pioneer of '49* (San Francisco: A. M. Robertson, 1923), pp. 101–02.

5. Fremont and Cora Older, *George Hearst, California Pioneer* (Los Angeles: Westernlore Press, 1966), pp. 148–49; and Leonard J. Arrington, "Abundance from the Earth: The Beginnings of Commercial Mining in Utah," *Utah Historical Quarterly* 31 (June 1963): 212–14. For a description of Hearst's acquisition of the Homestake, see Paul, *Mining Frontiers*, pp. 183–85.

6. Atherton, "Structure and Balance," pp. 55–66. For James F. Wardner, see Paul, *Mining Frontiers*, pp. 189–90; and Reed to Wardner, May 3, 1887, Letters and Private Papers of Simeon Gannett Reed, MS, 40 vols. Reed College, Portland, Ore.: vol. 23, pt. 1, 1886–89, p. 31 (hereafter cited as Reed Papers).

7. Charles C. Goodwin, *As I Remember Them* (Salt Lake City: Salt Lake Commercial Club, 1913), p. 202. For Sheedy, see Sheedy, *Autobiography*, pp. 21–22. William D. Mangam, *The Clarks, an*

American Phenomenon (New York: Silver Bow Press, 1941), pp. 16–30.

8. William Randolph Hearst, Jr., "The Frontier Life—Part 2," *San Francisco Examiner and Chronicle*, August 21, 1966. For a biographical sketch of Paul, see *Pacific Coast Annual Mining Review, 1888* (San Francisco: San Francisco Journal of Commerce Publishing Co., January 1889), p. 25.

9. Byers, *Biography of Colorado*, pp. 245–46; Jerome C. Smiley, *History of Denver, with Outlines of the Earlier History of the Rocky Mountain Country* (Denver: J. H. Williamson and Co., 1903), p. 566; and Waters, *Midas of the Rockies*, p. 339.

10. Bancroft, *Chronicles of the Builders*, 4: 214–24.

11. Lewis, *Silver Kings*, p. 156.

12. Kent Sheldon Larsen, "The Life of Thomas Kearns" (M.A. thesis, University of Utah, 1964), pp. 2–15.

13. Clipping from *Denver Post*, April 10, 1910, in Dawson, *Scrapbooks*, 23: 171.

14. The best secondary work on Sutro is Robert E. and Mary F. Stewart, *Adolph Sutro, a Biography* (Berkeley, Calif.: Howell-North, 1962), especially pp. 1–37. For Bela S. Buell, see Liston E. Leyendecker, "Bela Stevens Buell, Central City Entrepreneur (1836–1918)" (Ph.D. diss., University of Denver, 1966), pp. 20–41, 143, 254.

15. Sheedy, *Autobiography*, p. 49.

16. Ibid., pp. 51–52.

17. John Hays Hammond, *The Autobiography of John Hays Hammond*, 2 vols. (New York: Farrar and Rinehart, 1935), 1: 61.

18. Ibid., pp. 147–48.

19. Hill to wife, March 22, 1865, folio 2, notebook 2, Hill Papers. See biography of Hill in Bancroft, *Chronicles of the Builders*, 4: 377–98. Also see Jesse D. Hale, "The First Successful Smelter in Colorado," *Colorado Magazine* 13 (September 1936): 161–67; and Fell, "Nathaniel P. Hill," pp. 315–32; Alonzo E. Ellsworth, "Early Denver Business," *Denver Westerners' Brand Book* 4 (1950): 259; and Johnson, Malone, et al., *Dictionary of American Biography*, 9: 43.

20. Lloyd Tevis, "Industrial and Financial Growth of California and the West," *Pony Express* 16 (June 1949): 10–11.

21. J. A. Burkhart, "The Frontier Merchant and Social History," *Montana Magazine of History* 2 (October 1952): 8.

22. Paul, "My First Two Years," p. 45.

23. Ibid., p. 45.

24. Ibid., pp. 50–53; and Leigh H. Irvine, ed., *A History of the New California, Its Resources and People*, 2 vols. (New York: Lewis Publishing Co., 1905), 2: 672.

25. Lewis C. Gandy, *The Tabors: A Footnote of Western History* (New York: Press of the Pioneers, 1934), pp. 188–91. For a more recent account of Tabor's early mining ventures, see Duane A. Smith, *Horace Tabor, His Life and the Legend* (Boulder: Colorado Associated University Press, 1973), pp. 59–78.

26. Burkhart, "The Frontier Merchant," pp. 5–6; *Dictionary of American Biography*, 13: 612.

27. Tabor, "Cabin Life," p. 6.

28. Smiley, *History of Denver*, p. 809.

29. Tevis, "Industrial and Financial Growth," p. 10.

30. C. B. Glasscock, *The War of the Copper Kings, the Builders of Butte and the Wolves of Wall Street* (New York: Grosset and Dunlap, 1966), p. 59.

31. Hakola, "Samuel T. Hauser and the Economic Development of Montana," pp. 80–81, 83.

32. Ibid., pp. 85–86.

33. Mangam, *The Clarks*, pp. 45–46; and Thomas A. Rickard, *A History of American Mining* (New York: American Institute of Mining Engineers, 1932), p. 357.

34. Julian Dana, *The Man Who Built San Francisco: A Study of Ralston's Journey with Banners* (New York: Macmillan Co., 1936), pp. 231–32; David Lavender, *Nothing Seemed Impossible: William C. Ralston and Early San Francisco* (Palo Alto, Calif.: American West Publishing Co., 1975), pp. 186–87, 232–35; and Eliot Lord, *Comstock Mining and Miners* (Berkeley, Calif.: Howell-North, 1959), pp. 246–47.

35. Angel, *History of Nevada*, p. 594.

36. Joseph H. Cash, "Labor in the West: The Homestake Mining Company and Its Workers, 1877–1942" (Ph.D. diss., University of Iowa, 1966), pp. 30–31. Also see Cash, *Working the Homestake* (Ames: Iowa State University Press, 1973).

Chapter 4

1. Paul, *Mining Frontiers*, p. 10.

2. Bancroft, *Chronicles of the Builders*, 4: 243.

3. Paul, *Mining Frontiers*, pp. 76–78; Marye, *From '49 to '83 in California and Nevada*, pp. 124–25; and Samuel P. Davis, ed., *The History of Nevada*, 2 vols. (Reno, Nev.: Elms Publishing Co., 1913), 1: 415–16.

4. Dan De Quille, *The Big Bonanza* (New York: Alfred A. Knopf, 1967), p. 377; Paul, *Mining Frontiers*, pp. 78–80; and Bancroft, *Chronicles of the Builders*, 4: 200.

5. Angel, *History of Nevada*, unnumbered page facing p. 48.

6. Evalyn Walsh McLean, *Father Struck It Rich* (Boston: Little, Brown, and Co., 1936), p. 36.

7. Ibid., p. 40.

8. William S. Greever, *The Bonanza West: The Story of the Western Mining Rushes, 1848–1900* (Norman: University of Oklahoma Press, 1963), p. 222, 239; and Glasscock, *War of the Copper Kings*, pp. 83–84.

9. Harry M. Gorham, *My Memories of the Comstock* (Los Angeles: Suttonhouse Publishers, 1939), p. 23.

10. Goodwin, *As I Remember Them*, p. 60.

11. McCoy, *Historic Sketches of the Cattle Trade*, p. 395.

12. See statement by Walsh in the *Denver Post*, April 10, 1910; and Older, *George Hearst, California Pioneer*, p. 143.

13. Sarah Ann McNelis, "The Life of F. Augustus Heinze" (M.A. thesis, Montana State University, 1947), pp. 199–201.

14. Paul, *Mining Frontiers*, p. 74.

15. Gorham, *My Memories of the Comstock*, pp. 104–6; Paul, *Mining Frontiers*, p. 78; and Jesse D. Mason, *History of Amador County, California, with Illustrations and Biographical Sketches of Its Prominent Men and Pioneers* (Oakland, Calif.: Thompson and West, 1881), pp. 150–52. See Hubert H. Bancroft, "The Plymouth Consolidated Gold Mine," MS, 1886, Bancroft Library, University of California, Berkeley, for other consolidated properties owned by Hayward in California.

16. Paul, *Mining Frontiers*, pp. 79–80.

17. Ibid., p. 83.

18. Paul, p. 118; and Leyendecker, "Bela Stevens Buell," pp. 164–71, 225.

19. Older, *George Hearst, California Pioneer*, pp. 156–58; Cash, "Labor in the West," pp. 44–45, 50–51; and Hubert H. Bancroft, "Biography of George Hearst," n.d., MS, Bancroft Library, p. 385.

20. August C. Bolino, "The Role of Mining in the Economic Development of Idaho Territory," *Oregon Historical Quarterly* 59 (June 1958): 147.

21. Clement to Reed, January 11, 1890, Reed Papers, vol. 26, 1890–91, pp. 3–4. Also, for evidence of blackmailing see W. Turrentine Jackson, *Treasure Hill, Portrait of a Silver Mining Camp* (Tucson: University of Arizona Press, 1963), p. 110; and Lord, *Comstock Mining and Miners*, p. 132.

22. Interview for the *Denver Republican*, July 5, 1901.

23. P. O'Rourke to Reed, August 11, 1887, Reed Papers, vol. 21, 1887, p. 153.

24. Quoted in Larsen, "The Life of Thomas Kearns," p. 14.

25. Walsh to David Wegg, December 12, 1896, Evalyn Walsh-McLean Family Papers, Business Correspndence, 1887–1903, container 77, file 1896, Manuscript Division, Library of Congress, Washingtion, D.C. (hereafter cited as the Walsh Papers).

26. Jackson, *Treasure Hill*, p. 113.

27. Paul, *Mining Frontiers*, p. 170; and Jackson, *Treasure Hill*, p. 110.

28. Lord, *Comstock Mining and Miners*, pp. 98–99.

29. Davis, *History of Nevada*, 1: 317; Bancroft, *Chronicles of the Builders*, 4: 197–98; and Angel, *History of Nevada*, pp. 334–35.

30. Quoted in Davis, *History of Nevada*, 1: 391. For an interpretation of territorial justice which is more sympathetic to the Nevada judges, see Earl S. Pomeroy, *The Territories and the United States, 1861–1890: Studies in Colonial Administration* (Philadelphia: University of Pennsylvania Press, 1947), pp. 55–56.

31. Goodwin, *As I Remember Them*, p. 143.

32. Lord, *Comstock Mining and Miners*, p. 134.

33. Ibid., pp. 164–65.

34. Ibid., p. 180.

35. Paul, *Mining Frontiers*, p. 173.

36. Hammond, *Autobiography*, 1: 181–82. Also, see Clark Spence, "The Mining Engineers in the West," in *The American West: An Appraisal*, ed. Robert G. Ferris (Santa Fe: Museum of New Mexico Press, 1963), p. 105.

37. Reed Papers, vol. 24, 1889, p. 47.

38. Clement to Reed, January 11, 1890, ibid., vol. 26, 1890–1891, pp. 4–5.

39. Ibid., pp. 4–5.

40. Clement to Reed, August 3, 1889, ibid., vol. 24, 1889, p. 32.

41. Clement to Reed, August 27, 1889, ibid., pp. 42–43.

42. Clement to Reed December 23, 1889, ibid., pp. 115–16.

43. Reed to Beatty, March 18, 1891, ibid., vol. 30, 1889–95, p. 199.

44. Clement to Martin Winch (Reed's business secretary), September 4, 1891, ibid., vol. 26, 1890–91, p. 167.

45. Clement to Reed, November 3, 1889, ibid., vol. 24, 1889, p. 75.

46. Clement to Reed, December 18, 1889, ibid., p. 108.

47. Clement to Reed, December 6, 1889, ibid., p. 105.

48. Clement to Reed, March 23, 1890, ibid., vol. 26, 1890–91, pp. 76–77.

49. Ibid., vol. 30, 1889–95, pp. 134–35; and Donald M. Sutherland, "The Business Activities of Simeon G. Reed from 1880 through 1895" (B.A. thesis, Reed College, 1937), pp. 71–73.

50. Larsen, "The Life of Thomas Kearns," pp. 12–14, 23. For information on the structure of silver deposits, see Bancroft, *Chronicles of the Builders*, 4: 343.

51. Quoted in Frank L. Wentworth, *Aspen on the Roaring Fork*, ed. Francis B. Rizzari (Lakewood, Colo.: Francis B. Rizzari, 1950), p. 269.

52. *Mines and Mining Men of Colorado*, pp. 48–49.

53. Arguments for reform of the apex ruling were raised continually, most notably by the federal Public Land Commission which investigated the land laws in the western United States in the late 1870s. The commission reported that the apex law encouraged litigation. Mine owners obviously could agree, but Congress did not enact the changes proposed by the commission. See Paul, *Mining Frontiers*, pp. 174–75.

54. Reed to I. D. Haines, November 11, 1876, Reed Papers, vol. 7, 1872–77, pp. 240–42.

55. Older, *George Hearst, California Pioneer*, p. 142.

56. Ibid., p. 142.

57. Cecil G. Tilton, *William Chapman Ralston, Courageous Builder* (Boston: Christopher Publishing House, 1935), p. 210.

58. Sheedy, *Autobiography*, p. 44.

59. Reese, " 'Uncle Jesse,' " p. 30.

60. Stewart, *Adolph Sutro, a Biography*, p. 169.

61. Quoted in Archibald C. Unsworth, "Memoir," (material on Adolph Sutro), MS, vol. 1, Sutro Branch, California State Library, San Francisco, pp. ii, 39–40.

Chapter 5

1. See, for example, "The Coeur d'Alene Labor Troubles," a chapter in Greever's synthesis of the mining frontier, *The Bonanza West*, pp. 274–85; Robert W. Smith, *The Coeur d'Alene Mining War of 1892: A Case Study of an Industrial Dispute* (Corvallis: Oregon State University, 1961); Benjamin M. Rastall, *The Labor History of the Cripple Creek District: A Study in Industrial Evolution*, Economic and Political Series, vol. 3, no. 1 (Madison: University of Wisconsin Press, 1908); Stewart Holbrook's popular *The Rocky Mountain Revolution* (New York: Henry Holt and Co., 1956); and Melvyn Dubofsky, "The Origins of Western Working Class Radicalism 1890–1905," *Labor History* 7 (Spring 1966): 131–154; idem, "The Leadville Strike of 1896–1897: An Appraisal," *Mid-America* 48 (April 1966): 99–118; and idem, *We Shall Be All: A History of the Industrial Workers of the World* (Chicago: Quadrangle Books, 1969). For a recent interpretation of the militant labor movement as an outgrowth of the rapid

Notes 159

industrialization of the mines rather than of the lawlessness of the frontier, see Richard E. Lingenfelter, *The Hardrock Miners: A History of the Mining Labor Movement in the American West, 1863–1893* (Berkeley: University of California Press, 1974). For a further study of labor, see Joseph G. Rayback, *A History of American Labor* (New York: The Free Press, 1966), p. 234.

2. For an example of the popular treatment of frontier violence in the mining industry, see Bryce W. Anderson, "The Bomb at the Governor's Gate," *American West* 2 (Winter 1965): 12–21, 75–76.

3. Carl N. Degler, *The Age of the Economic Revolution, 1876–1900* (Glenview, Ill.: Scott, Foresman and Co., 1967), p. 132.

4. Dubofsky, "Western Working Class Radicalism," pp. 137–38; Vernon H. Jensen, *Heritage of Conflict: Labor Relations in the Nonferrous Metals Industry up to 1930* (Ithaca, N.Y.: Cornell University Press, 1950), pp. 39–40; Edwin P. Hoyt, *The Guggenheims and the American Dream* (New York: Funk and Wagnalls, 1967), pp. 171–72; and Atherton, "Structure and Balance in Western Mining History," pp. 81–84. The cyanide process extracted gold and silver from low-grade ores by treating them with a solution of sodium or potassium cyanide.

5. Joseph R. Conlin, *Big Bill Haywood and the Radical Union Movement* (Syracuse, N.Y.: Syracuse University Press, 1969), pp. 22–24.

6. Dubofsky, "Western Working Class Radicalism," p. 143.

7. Jensen, *Heritage of Conflict*, p. 27.

8. Goldsmith to Reed, June 6, 1887, Reed Papers, vol. 20, 1887, p. 96.

9. Jensen, *Heritage of Conflict*, pp. 28–29; and Smith, *The Coeur d'Alene Mining War*, p. 36.

10. Jensen, *Heritage of Conflict*, pp. 29–31; Hammond, *Autobiography*, 1: 186–89; and Smith, *The Coeur d'Alene Mining War*, pp. 34–37.

11. Smith, *The Coeur d'Alene Mining War*, pp. 41–46; and Hammond, *Autobiography*, 1: 189–91.

12. Hammond, *Autobiography*, 1: 191.

13. Smith, *The Coeur d'Alene Mining War*, pp. 61–84; and Jensen, *Heritage of Conflict*, pp. 34–36.

14. Smith, *The Coeur d'Alene Mining War*, p. 50.

15. Ibid., pp. 85–122; and Jensen, *Heritage of Conflict*, pp. 36–37.

16. Hammond, *Autobiography*, 2: 700.

17. Ibid., p. 699. Hammond apparently equated the I.W.W. with the W.F.M.

18. Ibid., p. 52.
19. Spence, "The Mining Engineers in the West," p. 109.
20. Quoted in Jensen, *Heritage of Conflict*, pp. 111–12. For Grant's reaction to a similar strike in 1899, see the *Colorado Springs Gazette*, July 11, July 12, and August 16, 1899.
21. Irving Howbert, *Memories of a Lifetime in the Pikes Peak Region* (New York: G. P. Putnam's Sons, 1925), p. 271. For a description of the Cripple Creek strike, see Marshall Sprague, *Money Mountain: The Story of Cripple Creek Gold* (Boston: Little, Brown and Co., 1953), pp. 133–56.
22. Howbert, *Lifetime in the Pikes Peak Region*, p. 272.
23. Ibid., pp. 273–77. For Populism, see Dubofsky, "Western Working Class Radicalism," pp. 140–42.
24. For the Cripple Creek Strike, see Sprague, *Money Mountain*, p. 154. For the Coeur d'Alene strike, see Jensen, *Heritage of Conflict*, p. 72.
25. Sheedy, *Autobiography*, pp. 49–50. Mining entrepreneurs were not always as generous as Sheedy. As mining became increasingly mechanized, mine accidents proliferated. Nonetheless, many owners, often absentee, showed an extraordinary reluctance to spend money on the health and safety of their employees. From 1860 to 1910, asphyxiation by dynamite gas, silicosis from machine drills' dust, falls from fast-moving mine cages, electrocutions, and other industrial tragedies left a heavy toll of miners dead, maimed, or injured. Often faced with inadequate compensation from owners, mine workers turned to their labor unions and to the political arena for protection. See Mark Wyman, "Industrial Revolution in the West: Hard-Rock Miners and the New Technology," *Western Historical Quarterly* 5 (January 1974): 39–57; and idem, "The Underground Miner, 1860–1910: Labor and Industrial Change in the Northern Rockies" (Ph.D. diss., University of Washington, 1971), pp. 176–319.
26. Sheedy, *Autobiography*, pp. 49–50.
27. Cash, "Labor in the West," pp. 74–86, 152–165, 171. For a discussion of medical and educational services, pp. 165–175. Also see Winifred Black Bonfils, *The Life and Personality of Phoebe Apperson Hearst* (San Francisco: John Henry Nash, 1928), pp. 57–58; and Cash, "Labor in the West," p. 248. The lockout occurred in 1909 when the W.F.M. tried to impose the closed shop.
28. Walsh to Wegg, July 10, 1894, Walsh Papers, container 77, file 1894.
29. *Rocky Mountain News* (Denver), April 9, 1910.
30. *National Cyclopedia of American Biography*, 51 vols. (New York: James T. White and Co., 1892–1969), 15: 191. For a complete

description of Walsh's boarding house, see *Denver Republican*, April 9, 1910. Also, see McLean, *Father Struck It Rich*, pp. 61–62.

31. *Daily Alta California* (San Francisco), January 13, 1877.

32. Quoted in Conlin, *Big Bill Haywood*, p. 15.

33. Ibid., pp. 14–16.

34. Charles M. Hough, "Leadville, Colorado, 1878–1898: A Study in Unionism" (M.A. thesis, University of Colorado, 1958), pp. 87–88.

35. Quoted in Jensen, *Heritage of Conflict*, p. 29.

36. Quoted in Dawson, *Scrapbooks*, 23: 529.

37. Jensen, *Heritage of Conflict*, pp. 41–42; and Sprague, *Money Mountain*, pp. 138–39, 148.

38. *Salt Lake Tribune*, October 19, 1918, p. 4; and Larsen, "The Life of Thomas Kearns," pp. 17, 20–21.

39. Larsen, "The Life of Thomas Kearns," p. 35.

40. A. G. MacKenzie, "Stories of Early Utah Mining Leaders," MS, 1925, Utah State Historical Society, Salt Lake City.

41. Larsen, "The Life of Thomas Kearns," p. 18.

42. For Mackay's reaction to a strike in Virginia City, Nevada, see Goodwin, *As I Remember Them*, p. 122.

43. Quoted in Drury, *An Editor on the Comstock Lode*, p. 65.

44. *Dictionary of American Biography*, 5: 46; Glasscock, *The War of the Copper Kings*, p. 118; and Norma Smith, "The Rise and Fall of the Butte Miners' Union, 1878–1914" (M.A. thesis, Montana State University, 1961), p. 23.

45. Quoted in Goodwin, *As I Remember Them*, p. 274.

46. Barrett, "Colonel E. A. Wall," pp. 3–6.

47. James B. Allen, "The Company Town: A Passing Phase of Utah's Industrial Development," *Utah Historical Quarterly* 34 (Spring 1966): 149–50; Reese, " 'Uncle Jesse,' " pp. 27–28; and Whitney, *History of Utah*, 4: 514. For a discussion of company-owned mining towns and some of their abuses, see James B. Allen, *The Company Town in the American West* (Norman: University of Oklahoma Press, 1966).

48. Knight to Superintendent John Roundy, December 16, 1908, Business Records and Family Papers of Jesse Knight, Knight Investment Company Correspondence, box 50, file Q–R, Brigham Young University Archives, Provo, Utah (hereafter cited as Knight Papers). Unless otherwise indicated, all citations refer to the Knight Investment Company Correspondence.

49. R. E. Allen, secretary of Knight Investment Co., to C. A. Williams, September 14, 1909, Knight Papers, box 51, file V–Z. For a description of the model coal-mining town owned by Knight, see Allen, "The Company Town," pp. 150–51.

50. Cash, "Labor in the West," p. 141.

51. Jensen, *Heritage of Conflict*, pp. 96–97; and Phelps, *California's Representative Men*, 1: 226.

52. Minar Shoebotham, *Anaconda: Life of Marcus Daly, the Copper King* (Harrisburg, Pa.: Stackpole Co., 1956), pp. 122, 191–200.

53. Smith, "Rise and Fall of the Butte Miners' Union," pp. 24–25; and Jensen, *Heritage of Conflict*, pp. 292–94.

54. Jensen, *Heritage of Conflict*, p. 291; and Smith, "Rise and Fall of the Butte Miners' Union," pp. 22, 37.

55. See James B. Allen, "The Company-Owned Mining Town in the West: Exploitation or Benevolent Paternalism?," in *Reflections of Western Historians: Papers of the 7th Annual Conference of the Western History Association, 1967*, ed. John A. Carroll (Tucson: University of Arizona Press, 1969), pp. 177–97.

56. Tabor, "Autobiography," p. 21.

Chapter 6

1. Marye, *From '49 to '83 in California and Nevada*, p. 66.

2. Harold Barger and Samuel H. Schurr, *The Mining Industries, 1899–1939: A Study of Output, Employment and Productivity* (New York: National Bureau of Economic Research, Inc., 1944), p. 101, n. 19.

3. McNelis, "Life of F. Augustus Heinze," p. 231; and Rickard, *A History of American Mining*, pp. 359–60.

4. Don L. and Jean H. Griswold, *The Carbonate Camp Called Leadville* (Denver: University of Denver Press, 1951), pp. 63–64.

5. Knight, *Jesse Knight Family*, pp. 38–41.

6. Lewis, *Silver Kings*, p. 43.

7. Larsen, "The Life of Thomas Kearns," p. 14.

8. Walsh to Wegg, August 2, 1894, Walsh Papers, container 77, file 1894.

9. Walsh to Wegg, March 6, 1895, ibid., file 1895.

10. Walsh to Wegg, June 10, 1895, ibid.

11. McCombe to Tabor, June 30, 1892, Horace A. W. Tabor Family Papers, file 81, no. 3, State Historical Society of Colorado, Denver (hereafter cited as Tabor Papers).

12. John Garraty, *The New Commonwealth, 1877–1890* (New York: Harper and Row, 1968), p. 97.

13. Angel, *History of Nevada*, p. 616.

14. Knight to Superintendent of the Mountain Lake Extension Mining Co., April 23, 1909, Knight Papers, box 48, file C.

15. R. E. Allen, secretary of the Knight Investment Co., to the Salt

Lake Stock and Mining Exchange, August 13, 1909, ibid., box 51, file S.

16. Secretary of the Big Hill Mining Co. to Raymond Knight, December 5, 1909, ibid., box 48, file C. Also, see secretary of the Copperfield Mining Co. to the Knight Investment Co., June 8, 1909, ibid.

17. R. E. Allen to E. L. Nolting, October 7, 1909, ibid., box 50, file N–O.

18. Knight to a fellow Mormon, March 16, 1909, ibid., box 48, file A–B.

19. See records of interest payments to the Zion's Saving Bank and Trust Company from the Knight Investment Co., ibid. For Simeon Reed, see D. E. Livingston-Little, "An Economic History of North Idaho—Discovery and Development of the Coeur d'Alene Mines," p. 5, *Journal of the West* 3 (July 1964): 330.

20. Martin Winch to Reed, December 29, 1893, Reed Papers, vol. 31, 1890–94, p. 241.

21. McNelis, "Life of F. Augustus Heinze," pp. 50–51; and Reed Papers, vol. 20, 1887, p. 129.

22. Walsh to Wegg, March 27, 1895, Walsh Papers, cont. 77, file 1895.

23. *White Pine News* (Ely, Nevada), August 21, 1869, as quoted in Jackson, *Treasure Hill*, p. 152.

24. For the Robert E. Lee, see Hough, "Leadville, Colorado, 1878–1898," pp. 14–19. The other five mines were the Little Pittsburg Consolidated, the Chrysolite, the Little Chief, the Iron Silver, and the Morning Star Consolidated. For the Kip and Buell Gold Company, see Leyendecker, "Bela Stevens Buell," pp. 84–121. Barrett, "When Big Money Came to Owyhee," pp. 4–5.

25. Hakola, "Samuel T. Hauser," pp. 87–88.

26. Ibid., pp. 72–73, 292.

27. Clark C. Spence, *British Investments and the American Mining Frontier, 1860–1901* (Ithaca, N.Y.: Cornell University Press, 1958), pp. 24, 51–56; and Lewis Atherton, "The Mining Promoter in the Trans-Mississippi West," *Western Historical Quarterly* 1 (January 1970): 38–40.

28. On one occasion Knight refused an offer to advertise his properties in the *Salt Lake Mining Review*. See secretary of the Knight Investment Co. to *Salt Lake Mining Review*, September 10, 1908, Knight Papers, box 51, file S.

29. B. R. McDonald to Knight Investment Co., August 12, 1908, ibid., box 50, file M.

30. Harry S. Lewis to Knight, October 5, 1909, ibid., box 49, file L.

31. Emmons to Tabor, February 17, 1881, U.S. Geological Survey, Emmons Copybook, Letters Sent, 1879–86, National Archives, Washington, D.C.

32. See Jackson, *Treasure Hill*, p. 171; and Spence, *British Investments*, p. 69.

33. Hill to wife, March 22, 1865, Hill Papers, folio 2, notebook 2.

34. Daly Mining Co., Utah Territory, *Annual Report*, 1888, p. 13. Also, see Clark C. Spence, *Mining Engineers and the American West: The Lace-Boot Brigade, 1849–1933* (New Haven, Conn.: Yale University Press, 1970), p. 266.

35. Stewart, *Adolph Sutro*, p. 49. For the relationship between Reed and Hammond, see Livingston-Little, "An Economic History of North Idaho," p. 330. Also, see Hammond to Reed, August 5, 1891, Reed Papers, vol. 33, 1891, p. 138.

36. W. P. Dunham, mining agent, to Walsh, 23 February 1903, *Walsh Papers*, cont. 77, file 1903.

37. Quoted in William R. Hearst, Jr., "A Mining Man's Early Day Story," *San Francisco Examiner and Chronicle*, September 4, 1966.

38. Knight to H. S. Lewis, October 9, 1909, Knight Papers, box 49, file L.

39. Knight to Ida Waseveyler, September 21, 1909, ibid., box 48, file A–B.

40. Walsh to Wegg, May 21, 1895, Walsh Papers, cont. 77, file 1895.

41. Hough, "Leadville, Colorado, 1878–1898," pp. 20–21; and G. Thomas Ingham, *Digging Gold among the Rockies* (Philadelphia: Hubbard Brothers, 1880), pp. 445–47.

42. Wilbur F. Stone, "Dictation and Related Biographical Material for David H. Moffat," MS, 1885, Bancroft Library, p. 3.

43. Lingenfelter, *The Hardrock Miners*, pp. 143–56.

44. Ingham, *Digging Gold among the Rockies*, p. 440.

45. Bancroft, Chronicles of the Builders, 5: 201.

46. Angel, *History of Nevada*, p. 594.

47. Gilman M. Ostrander, *Nevada, the Great Rotten Borough, 1859–1964* (New York: Alfred A. Knopf, 1966), pp. 14–15, 52; and Bancroft, *Chronicles of the Builders*, 4: 17, 140.

48. Almarin B. Paul, *Paul's Electro-Chemical Dry Amalgamating Barrell Process* (San Francisco: Spaulding and Barto, 1872), pp. unnumbered.

49. S. F. Emmons to Clarence King, October 10, 1880, U.S. Geological Survey, *First Annual Report*, 1880, p. 63, as quoted in Thomas G. Manning, *Government in Science: The U.S. Geological*

Survey, 1867–1894 (Lexington: University of Kentucky Press, 1967), p. 63.

50. Hammond, *Autobiography*, 2: 579.

51. Hoyt, *The Guggenheims and the American Dream*, p. 145; Isaac F. Marcosson, *Metal Magic: The Story of the American Smelting and Refining Company* (New York: Farrar, Straus, and Co., 1949), pp. 59–60; and *History of the Arkansas Valley, Colorado* (Chicago: O. L. Baskin and Co., 1881), p. 234. The Little Pittsburg that "should have been stocked for two millions was stocked at twenty."

52. Angel, *History of Nevada*, p. 620.

53. See Manning, *Government in Science*, p. 63.

54. Rossiter W. Raymond, *Report on the Mineral Resources of the United States and Territories*, 3rd Annual Report, 1868 (Washington, D.C., 1869), p. 51.

55. Lord, *Comstock Mining and Miners*, p. 32.

56. Angel, *History of Nevada*, p. 536.

57. See Emmons to Tabor, February 17, 1881, U.S. Geological Survey, Emmons Copybook. Emmons was denied permission to inspect a Leadville mine in which Tabor evidently held an interest. He remarked: "As well as I can understand it, the question of my entering the mine, seems to be a personal difference between me and certain of the owners here, and the final refusal of permission to enter the mine, may absolve itself into the question as to which is the more worthy of public confidence, they or I."

58. Older, *George Hearst*, pp. 135–36; Bancroft, *Chronicles of the Builders*, 4: 134–35; Manning, *Government in Science*, p. 109.

59. Hammond, *Autobiography*, 2: 563.

60. Knight to Congressman Joseph Howell, April 7, 1908, Knight Papers, box 49, file H.

61. Manning, *Government in Science*, pp. 60, 70.

62. Rickard, *History of American Mining*, p. 133. See also Manning, *Government in Science*, p. 107.

63. U.S. Geological Survey to Knight, January 14, 1909, Knight Papers, box 49, file H; and H. H. Gilfry to Reed, December 13, 1887, Reed Papers, vol. 20, 1887, p. 199.

64. *National Cyclopedia of American Biography*, 26: 46. In 1919, the organization became the American Institute of Mining and Metallurgical Engineers. See also Reed Papers, vol. 31, 1890–94, p. 127.

65. Knight, *The Jesse Knight Family*, pp. 95–96. For Walsh and Hammond, see *National Cyclopedia of American Biography*, 15: 191; 26: 46.

66. Paul, *Mining Frontiers*, p. 132.

67. Wardner to Reed, May 6, 1887, Reed Papers, vol. 21, 1887, p. 64.

68. Linderman to Reed, May 25, 1887, ibid., p. 92.

69. See Hammond, *Autobiography*, 1:83–85. Also, see Spence, "The Mining Engineers in the West," p. 102.

70. Hearst, "A Mining Man's Early Day Story," *San Francisco Examiner and Chronicle*, September 4, 1966.

71. Sheedy, *Autobiography*, p. 51.

72. Quoted in Dawson, *Life and Character of Edward Oliver Wolcott*, 1:261.

73. Spence, "The Mining Engineers in the West," p. 102; Hammond, *Autobiography*, 1: 147–48; B.C. Forbes, *Men Who Are Making America* (New York: B.C. Forbes Publishing Co., 1922), p. 186; and Spence, *Mining Engineers and the American West*, pp. 72–73, 76–77.

74. Drury, *An Editor on the Comstock Lode*, p. 69.

75. Hammond, *Autobiography*, 1: 39. The fact that bogus mining engineers often were self-styled professors in part explains Hammond's concern.

76. Quoted in Spence, *Mining Engineers and the American West*, p. 70.

77. Ibid., p. 74.

78. For W. H. Patton, see Angel, *History of Nevada*, pp. 611–12. For Walter B. Devereux, see Bancroft, *Chronicles of the Builders*, 6: 635–36; for Haggin, see Hammond, *Autobiography*, 2: 514.

79. Henry Wolcott, "Dictation and Related Biographical Material for David H. Moffat," MS, 1885, Bancroft Library, p. 4.

80. Gorham, *My Memories of the Comstock*, p. 26.

81. Angel, *History of Nevada*, p. 574.

82. Spence, *Mining Engineers and the American West*, p. 244; *National Cyclopedia of American Biography*, 20: 145; *Dictionary of American Biography*, 13: 461; and Gary B. Hansen, "Industry of Destiny: Copper in Utah," *Utah Historical Quarterly* 31 (Summer 1963): 278–79.

83. Spence, "Mining Engineers in the West," pp. 110–11.

84. Gorham, *My Memories of the Comstock*, pp. 114–17.

85. *National Cyclopedia of American Biography*, 28: 257–58.

86. Cash, "Labor in the West," pp. 107–10; and Spence, *Mining Engineers and the American West*, p. 241.

87. Clement to Reed, January 20, 1888, Reed Papers, vol. 25, 1887–88, p. 90.

88. Thomas Egleston, *The Boston and Colorado Smelting Works* (Philadelphia: Sherman and Co., 1877), p. 18.

89. *Dictionary of American Biography*, 9: 43; and Frank Hall,

History of the State of Colorado, 4 vols. (Chicago: Blakely Printing Co., 1889–1895), 1: 443–47.

90. Knight to Duncan MacVichie, March 2, 1909, Knight Papers, box 50, file M.

91. Cash, "Labor in the West," p. 249.

92. Letter to Reed, July 7, 1887, Reed Papers, vol. 22, 1887, p. 35A.

93. Walsh to Wegg, December 12, 1896, Walsh Papers, cont. 77, file 1896.

94. See Walsh's reply on letter, B. F. Hall to Walsh, March 2, 1903, ibid., file 1903.

95. For evidence of caution regarding the adoption of new technology by entrepreneurs in the iron and steel, textiles, machine tools, and electric power industries, see W. Paul Strassman, *Risk and Technological Innovation: American Manufacturing Methods during the Nineteenth Century* (Ithaca, N.Y.: Cornell University Press, 1959).

96. *Pacific Coast Annual Mining Review, 1888* (San Francisco: San Francisco Journal of Commerce Publishing Co., 1889), p. 25; and David Lavender, *The Rockies* (New York: Harper and Row, 1968), p. 248.

97. Quoted in Shoebotham, *Anaconda, Life of Marcus Daly*, p. 72. Also, see Goodwin, *As I Remember Them*, p. 271.

98. McNelis, "Life of F. Augustus Heinze," p. 57.

99. Fletcher W. Jordan, "Interview," MS, 1921, State Historical Society of Colorado, Denver, p. 2.

100. Walter Cheesman, "Dictation and Related Biographical Material for David H. Moffat," MS, 1885, Bancroft Library, p. 2.

Chapter 7

1. De Quille, *The Big Bonanza*, pp. 258–59.

2. Bancroft, *Chronicles of the Builders*, 4: 253; Leyendecker, "Bela Stevens Buell," pp. 210–211; and Bancroft, "The Plymouth Consolidated Gold Mine," pp. 2–3.

3. Cash, "Labor in the West," pp. 45–50.

4. Herbert E. Smyth to Knight, June 10, 1909, Ibex Mining Co. Correspondence, Knight Papers, box 132, file R–Z.

5. Lord, *Comstock Mining and Miners*, pp. 258–59, 322–323, 333. The "miner's inch" was the volume of water that would flow through a hole one inch square in ten hours. See Greever, *The Bonanza West*, p. 52.

6. *San Francisco Chronicle*, August 28, 1879. See also, Hubert H. Bancroft, "Bancroft Scraps, Educated Men of California," Biographies, vol. 30, Bancroft Library, pp. 60–61.

7. Lord, *Comstock Mining and Miners*, p. 351.

8. Ibid.

9. De Quille, *The Big Bonanza*, p. 178; Mary M. Farrell, "William Andrews Clark" (M.A. thesis, University of Washington, 1933), p. 24; and Shoebotham, *Anaconda, Life of Marcus Daly*, pp. 98–102.

10. Shoebotham, pp. 88–89; and Hakola, "Samuel T. Hauser," pp. 280–81. See also *Rocky Mountain News*, September 2, 1879.

11. Quoted in Hakola, "Samuel T. Hauser," p. 281.

12. *San Francisco Chronicle*, August 28, 1879. Also, see Bancroft, *Bancroft Scraps, Educated Men of California*, 30: 60–61.

13. Hakola, "Samuel T. Hauser," pp. 283–86.

14. *National Cyclopedia of American Biography*, 15: 61; and Gandy, *The Tabors*, p. 211.

15. Hall, *America's Successful Men of Affairs*, 1: 723. See also Bancroft, *Chronicles of the Builders*, 6: 636–37.

16. Hall, *America's Successful Men of Affairs*, 1:724; and Bancroft, *Chronicles of the Builders*, 6: 640–41.

17. Paul, *Mining Frontiers*, p. 50. For the Hendey and Meyer Engineering Company, see Andrew Hensley, *Denver: Pencil Sketches and Graver Strokes* (Denver: Republican Publishing Co., 1886), p. 96. For Lloyd Tevis, see *Dictionary of American Biography*, 18: 385. For Knight's Supply Company, see Inter-Mountain Selling Co. to Knight Supply Co., December 5, 1908, Knight Papers, box 49, file I–J; and Knight to David Evans, August 11, 1908, Knight Papers, box 48, file E–F. For Andrew Jackson Davis, see E. G. Leipheimer, *The First National Bank of Butte: Seventy-Five Years of Continuous Banking Operation 1877 to 1952 under the Successive Ownership and Management of Three Men Each Named Andrew Jackson Davis* (Butte, Mont.: First National Bank of Butte, 1952), pp. 7–9, 47.

18. O. H. Harker to David Moffat, April 5, 1885, comp. Agnes W. Spring, Notes and Extracts from the Personal Papers of David H. Moffat and Jerome B. Chaffee, MS, State Historical Society of Colorado, Denver.

19. Clement to Reed, February 1, 1888, Reed Papers, vol. 25, 1887–88, p. 94.

20. U.S. Army Corps of Engineers, *Preliminary Report concerning Explorations and Surveys Principally in Nevada and Arizona, 1871* (Washington, D.C.: Government Printing Office, 1872), p. 56.

21. Ibid., p. 58.

22. Knight to Anders Mortensen, August 28, 1908, Knight Papers, box 50, file M.

23. For Joseph DeLamar, see Barrett, "When Big Money Came to

Owyhee," pp. 2–9, 20–29; for the Virginia and Truckee Railroad, see Stewart, *Adolph Sutro*, pp. 72–74; and Gilbert H. Kneiss, *Bonanza Railroads* (Stanford, Calif.: Stanford University Press, 1941), pp. 62–64.

24. Lord, *Comstock Mining and Miners*, pp. 254–55.

25. J. Carl Brogdon, "The History of Jerome, Arizona" (M.A. thesis, University of Arizona, 1952), pp. 16–18, 23–24.

26. Bancroft, *Chronicles of the Builders*, 6: 640; *Mines and Mining Men of Colorado*, p. 42; Wentworth, *Aspen on the Roaring Fork*, pp. 44–45; and Robert F. Bartlett, "Aspen, Colorado: The Mining Community, 1879–1893," *Denver Westerners Brand Book* 6 (1950): 147–51.

27. *Dictionary of American Biography*, 13: 75; Ellsworth, "Early Denver Business," p. 261; and McMechen, *The Moffat Tunnel of Colorado*, 1: 76–77.

28. Hakola, "Samuel T. Hauser," pp. 154, 158–159, 174–176, 264–265, 287–288. In 1908, Knight secured a rebate on a carload of timbers sent to his mines in the Tintic district. See Knight Investment Co. to J. F. Maginness, August 28, 1908, Knight Papers, box 50, file M.

29. Livingston-Little, "An Economic History of North Idaho," p. 329.

30. Reed to A. W. Geist, February 11, 1888, Reed Papers, vol. 23, pt. 1, 1886–89, p. 170.

31. Howbert, *My Memories of Pikes Peak*, pp. 282–83; and *Colorado Springs Gazette*, November 14, 1902, clipping in Dawson, *Scrapbooks*, 59: 285.

32. Howbert, *Memories of Pikes Peak*, p. 285.

33. Brogdon, "History of Jerome, Arizona," p. 26–27. See also Hall, *History of Colorado*, 1: 443–47; Gunther Barth, "Metropolism and Urban Elites in the Far West," in *The Age of Industrialism in America: Essays in Social Structure and Cultural Values*, ed. Frederic C. Jaher (New York: Free Press, 1968), p. 174; and Hensley, *Denver*, p. 97.

34. Leyendecker, "Bela Stevens Buell," p. 205. For the advantages and problems of tramway service in Nevada's White Pine mining district in the 1870s, see Jackson, *Treasure Hill*, pp. 177–78. For Wheeler, see Muriel S. Wolle, *Stampede to Timberline: The Ghost Towns and Mining Camps of Colorado* (Denver: Sage Books, 1949), p. 234. For Walsh, see McLean, *Father Struck It Rich*, p. 62.

35. Larsen, "The Life of Thomas Kearns," p. 21.

36. *Mines and Mining Men of Colorado*, pp. 71–72; and *Dictionary of American Biography*, 13: 75.

37. *San Francisco Chronicle*, August 28, 1879. Also, see Bancroft, *Bancroft Scraps, Educated Men of California*, 30: 60–61.

38. Paul, *Mining Frontiers*, p. 84.

39. Sprague, *Money Mountain*, p. 312, note 1.

40. For Grant, see Waters, *Midas of the Rockies*, p. 163; and Griswold, *The Carbonate Camp Called Leadville*, p. 66. For Knight, see Business Manager of the Ibex Gold Mining Co. to John Smith, December 2, 1909; letters to the Ibex Gold Mining Co. and the Utah Ore Sampling Co., July 14, 1913 and March 29, 1915, Ibex Mining Co. Correspondence, Knight Papers, box 132, file R–Z; and Knight Investment Company's Mining Records, Knight Papers, box 169, 1907–28.

41. Clement to Reed, November 4, 1887, Reed Papers, vol. 25, 1887–1888, p. 54.

42. Clement to Reed, February 7, 1888, ibid., pp. 95–96.

43. See ibid., vol. 23, pt. 2, 1886–89, pp. 344–45, 374–75, 400–401.

44. Reed to Clement, March 3, 1890, ibid., vol. 30, 1889–95, p. 69.

45. Livingston-Little, "An Economic History of North Idaho," pp. 324; 352, n. 425.

46. Glasscock, *The War of the Copper Kings*, p. 71. See also Mangam, *The Clarks*, p. 53.

47. Knight, *The Jesse Knight Family*, pp. 45–46. See also Hakola, "Samuel T. Hauser," pp. 272–73; Walsh to Wegg, September 28, and November 27, 1896, Walsh Papers, cont. 77, file 1896; and Wolcott, "Dictations for David H. Moffat," p. 5.

48. Walsh to Wegg, August 22, 1894, Walsh Papers, cont. 77, file 1894.

49. Hakola, "Samuel T. Hauser," p. 268; Reed Papers, vol. 28, 1889, pp. 149–51. See also Bancroft, *Chronicles of the Builders*, 4: 384–86; and Hall, *History of Colorado*, 1: 443–47.

50. Quoted in Barth, "Metropolism and Urban Elites," p. 174.

51. *Pacific Coast Annual Mining Review, 1888*, p. 68; *Mines and Mining Men of Colorado*, pp. 42–43; and Farrell, "William Andrews Clark," pp. 25, 27.

52. Cash, "Labor in the West," p. 114–15.

53. Articles of Incorporation, Tabor Mines and Mills Co., Tabor Papers, folio 329, nos. 1–5.

54. Alfred D. Chandler, Jr., *Strategy and Structure; Chapters in the History of the Industrial Enterprise* (Garden City, N.Y.: Doubleday and Co., 1966), pp. 29, 40–41. See also idem, "The Beginnings of 'Big Business' in American Industry," *Business History Review* 33 (Spring 1959): 1–31.

55. Knight, *The Jesse Knight Family*, pp. 65–66; and Stockholders of Record, Great Western Gold and Copper Mining Company, August 24, 1910, Company Correspondence, Knight Papers, box 110, file A–Z. See also Hakola, "Samuel T. Hauser," pp. 289–94.

56. Hakola, p. 294.

Chapter 8

1. Ray Allen Billington, *Westward Expansion: A History of the American Frontier* (New York: Macmillan Co., 1967), p. 684.

BIBLIOGRAPHY

Manuscripts

Brigham Young University Archives, Provo, Utah
  Business Records and Family Papers of Jesse Knight
California State Library, Sutro Branch, San Francisco, California
  Memoir (by Archibald C. Unsworth). Material on Adolph Sutro.
    Vol. 1. Unsworth was Sutro's traveling companion and secretary.
Library of Congress, Manuscript Division, Washington, D.C.
  Evalyn Walsh McLean Family Papers, 1886–1948. Mrs. McLean
    was the daughter of Thomas Walsh. The Papers contain his
    business correspondence, 1887–1903.
National Archives, Washington, D.C.
  U.S. Geological Survey, Emmons Copybook, Letters Sent, 1879–86.
    Samuel F. Emmons to H.A.W. Tabor, February 17, 1881.
Reed College, Portland, Oregon
  Letters and Private Papers of Simeon G. Reed. Reed College Proj-
    ect, Divison of Professional and Service Projects, W.P.A., 1940.
    40 volumes.
State Historical Society of Colorado, Denver, Colorado
  Horace A.W. Tabor Family Papers
  Interview with Fletcher W. Jordan, July 30, 1921. Jordan was the
    step-son of Jerome Chaffee's mining partner, Eben Smith.
  Nathaniel P. Hill Papers
  Notes and Extracts from the Personal Papers of David H. Moffat
    and Jerome B. Chaffee (by Agnes W. Spring, compiler). The
    original complete collection of the Moffat-Chaffee Papers is in the
    First National Bank, Denver.
  Scrapbooks (by Thomas F. Dawson). Clippings from Colorado
    newspapers collected by the former director of the Historical
    Society.
University of California, Bancroft Library, Berkeley, California
  Autobiography (by Horace A.W. Tabor), 1889.

"Bancroft Scraps, Educated Men of California" (by Hubert H. Bancroft), n.d.

Cabin Life in Colorado (by Augusta Tabor), 1884.

Dictation and Related Biographical Material for David H. Moffat (by Walter Cheesman), 1885; (by Wilbur F. Stone), 1885; and (by Henry R. Wolcott), 1885.

The Plymouth Consolidated Gold Mine (by Hubert H. Bancroft), 1886.

Utah State Historical Society, Salt Lake City, Utah
Stories of Early Utah Mining Leaders (by A.G. MacKenzie), 1925.

Newspapers

Various newspapers provided obituaries or interviews of the bonanza kings as well as other kinds of editorial comment:

Colorado Springs Gazette. July 11, 12, August 16, 1899; November 14, 1902.

Daily Alta California (San Francisco). January 13, 1877.

Denver Polly Pry. 1914.

Denver Post. April 21, 1907; April 10, 1910.

Denver Republican. July 5, 1901; April 9, 1910.

New York Times. December 2, 1918.

Rocky Mountain News (Denver). September 2, 1879; April 9, 1910.

Salt Lake Tribune (Salt Lake City). October 19, 1918.

San Francisco Chronicle. August 28, 1879.

San Francisco Examiner and Chronicle. August 21, September 4, 1966.

Contemporary Books, Journals, and Reports

Angel, Myron. *History of Nevada with Illustrations and Biographical Sketches of Its Prominent Men and Pioneers.* Berkeley, Calif.: Howell-North, 1958. Originally published, 1881.

Bancroft, Hubert H. *Chronicles of the Builders of the Commonwealth.* 7 vols. San Francisco: History Co., 1891–92.

"Biographical Sketches." In *Pacific Coast Annual Mining Review, 1888*, pp. 23–39. San Francisco: San Francisco Journal of Commerce Publishing Co., 1889.

Daly Mining Company, Utah Territory. *Annual Report*, January 1, 1888, to January 1, 1889. Bancroft Library.

De Quille, Dan. *The Big Bonanza.* New York: Alfred A. Knopf, 1967. Originally published, 1876.

Egleston, Thomas. *The Boston and Colorado Smelting Works.* Philadelphia: Sherman and Co., 1877.

Hall, Frank. *History of the State of Colorado.* 4 vols. Chicago: Blakely Printing Co., 1889–95.

Hall, Henry, ed. *America's Successful Men of Affairs: An Encyclopedia of Contemporaneous Biography.* 2 vols. New York: New York Tribune, 1895–96.

Hensley, Andrew. *Denver: Pencil Sketches and Graver Strokes.* Denver: Republican Publishing Co., 1886.

Ingham, G. Thomas. *Digging Gold among the Rockies.* Philadelphia: Hubbard Brothers, 1880.

Kelly, J. Wells, comp. *First Directory of Nevada Territory, 1862.* Los Gatos, Calif.: Talisman Press, 1962. Originally published, 1862.

Lord, Eliot. *Comstock Mining and Miners.* Berkeley, Calif.: Howell-North, 1959. Originally published, 1883.

Mason, Jesse D. *History of Amador County, California, with Illustrations and Biographical Sketches of Its Prominent Men and Pioneers.* Oakland, Calif.: Thompson and West, 1881.

McCoy, Joseph G. *Historic Sketches of the Cattle Trade of the West and Southwest.* Kansas City, Mo.: Ramsey, Millett and Hudson, 1874.

Mines and Mining Men of Colorado, Historical, Descriptive and Pictorial; an Account of the Principal Producing Mines of Gold and Silver. Denver: J. G. Canfield, 1893.

Paul, Almarin B. *Paul's Electro-Chemical Dry Amalgamating Barrell Process.* San Francisco: Spaulding and Barto, 1872.

Phelps, Alonzo. *Contemporary Biography of California's Representative Men.* 2 vols. San Francisco: A. L. Bancroft and Co., 1881.

Raymond, Rossiter W. *Report on the Mineral Resources of the United States and Territories.* 3rd Annual Report, 1868. Washington, D.C.: Government Printing Office, 1869.

Tevis, Lloyd. "Industrial and Financial Growth of California and the West." *Pony Express* 15 (January 1949): 3–4, 14; 16 (June 1949): 3–6, 8–11. Reprint of an address before the American Bankers Association, 1881.

U.S. Army, Corps of Engineers. *Preliminary Report concerning Explorations and Surveys Principally in Nevada and Arizona, 1871.* Washington, D.C., 1872.

Whitney, Orson F. *History of Utah.* 4 vols. Salt Lake City: George Q. Cannon and Sons, 1892–1904.

Published Memoirs and Reminiscent Accounts

Dawson, Thomas F. *Life and Character of Edward Oliver Wolcott, Late a Senator of the United States from the State of Colorado.* 2 vols. New York: Knickerbocker Press, 1911.

Drury, Wells. *An Editor on the Comstock Lode.* New York: Farrar and Rinehart, 1936.

Goodwin, Charles C. *As I Remember Them.* Salt Lake City: Salt Lake Commercial Club, 1913.

Gorham, Harry M. *My Memories of the Comstock.* Los Angeles: Suttonhouse Publishers, 1939.

Hammond, John Hays. *The Autobiography of John Hays Hammond.* 2 vols. New York: Farrar and Rinehart, 1935.

Howbert, Irving. *Memories of a Lifetime in the Pikes Peak Region.* New York: G.P. Putnam's Sons, 1925.

Marye, George T., Jr. *From '49 to '83 in California and Nevada, Chapters from the Life of George Thomas Marye, A Pioneer of '49.* San Francisco: A.M. Robertson, 1923.

McLean, Evalyn Walsh. *Father Struck It Rich.* Boston: Little, Brown and Co., 1936.

Paul, Almarin B. "My First Two Years in California." *Quarterly of the Society of California Pioneers* 4 (March 1927): 22–54.

Sheedy, Dennis. *The Autobiography of Dennis Sheedy.* Denver: privately printed, 1922.

Wentworth, Frank L. *Aspen on the Roaring Fork.* Edited by Francis B. Rizzari. Lakewood, Colo.: Francis B. Rizzari, 1950. Originally published, 1935.

Theses and Dissertations

Brogdon, J. Carl. "The History of Jerome, Arizona." M.A. thesis, University of Arizona, 1952.

Cash, Joseph H. "Labor in the West: The Homestake Mining Company and its Workers, 1877–1942." Ph.D. dissertation, University of Iowa, 1966.

Farrell, Mary M. "William Andrews Clark." M.A. thesis, University of Washington, 1933.

Hakola, John W. "Samuel T. Hauser and the Economic Development of Montana: A Case Study in Nineteenth-Century Frontier Capitalism." Ph.D. dissertation, Indiana University, 1961.

Hough, Charles M. "Leadville, Colorado, 1878–1898: A Study in Unionism." M.A. thesis, University of Colorado, 1958.

Larsen, Kent S. "The Life of Thomas Kearns." M.A. thesis, University of Utah, 1964.

Leyendecker, Liston E. "Bela Stevens Buell, Central City Entrepreneur (1836–1918)." Ph.D. dissertation, University of Denver, 1966.

McNelis, Sarah Ann. "The Life of F. Augustus Heinze." M.A. thesis, Montana State University, 1947.

Reese, Gary F. " 'Uncle Jesse,' The Story of Jesse Knight, Miner, Industrialist, Philanthropist." M.S. thesis, Brigham Young University, 1961.

Smith, Norma. "The Rise and Fall of the Butte Miners' Union, 1878–1914." M.A. thesis, Montana State University, 1961.

Sutherland, Donald M. "The Business Activities of Simeon G. Reed from 1880 through 1895." B.A. thesis, Reed College, 1937.

Wyman, Mark. "The Underground Miner, 1860–1910: Labor and Industrial Change in the Northern Rockies." Ph.D. dissertation, University of Washington, 1971.

Secondary Articles and Books

Akers, Dwight. "David H. Moffat and His Home Town." *Colorado Magazine* 27 (July 1950): 212–14.

Allen, James B. "The Company-Owned Mining Town in the West: Exploitation or Benevolent Paternalism?" In *Reflections of Western Historians: Papers of the 7th Annual Conference of the Western History Association, 1967,* edited by John A. Carroll, pp. 177–97. Tucson: University of Arizona Press, 1969.

———. "The Company Town: A Passing Phase of Utah's Industrial Development." *Utah Historical Quarterly* 34 (Spring 1966): 138–160.

———. *The Company Town in the American West.* Norman: University of Oklahoma Press, 1966.

Anderson, Bryce W. "The Bomb at the Governor's Gate." *American West* 2 (Winter 1965): 12–21, 75–76.

Arrington, Leonard J. "Abundance from the Earth: The Beginnings of Commercial Mining in Utah." *Utah Historical Quarterly* 31 (June 1963): 192–219.

Atherton, Lewis. *The Cattle Kings.* Bloomington: Indiana University Press, 1961.

———. "The Mining Promoter in the Trans-Mississippi West." *Western Historical Quarterly* 1 (January 1970): 35–50.

———. "Structure and Balance in Western Mining History." *Huntington Library Quarterly* 30 (November 1966): 55–84.

Barger, Harold, and Schurr, Samuel H. *The Mining Industries, 1899–1939: A Study of Output, Employment and Productivity*. New York: National Bureau of Economic Research, Inc., 1944.

Barrett, G. W. "Colonel E. A. Wall: Mines, Miners, and Mormons." *Idaho Yesterdays* 14 (Fall 1970): 3–11.

―――. "Enos Andrew Wall, Mine Superintendent and Inventor." *Idaho Yesterdays* 15 (Spring 1971): 24–31.

―――. "When Big Money Came to Owyhee." *Idaho Yesterdays* 13 (Spring 1969): 2–9, 22–29.

Barth, Gunther. *Bitter Strength: A History of the Chinese in the United States, 1850–1870*. Cambridge, Mass.: Harvard University Press, 1964.

―――. "Metropolism and Urban Elites in the Far West." In *The Age of Industrialism in America: Essays in Social Structure and Cultural Values*, edited by Frederic C. Jaher, pp. 158–87. New York: Free Press, 1968.

Bartlett, Robert F. "Aspen, Colorado: The Mining Community, 1879–1893." *Denver Westerners Brand Book* 6 (1950): 131–60.

Baur, John E. "Early Days and California Years of John Percival Jones, 1849–1867." *Southern California Quarterly* 44 (June 1962): 97–131.

Billington, Ray Allen. *Westward Expansion: A History of the American Frontier*. New York: Macmillan Co., 1967.

Biographical Record of Salt Lake City and Vicinity. Chicago: National Historical Record Co., 1902.

Blackburn, George, and Richards, Sherman, Jr. "A Demographic History of the West: Manistee County, Michigan, 1860." *Journal of American History* 57 (December 1970): 600–618.

Bolino, August C. "The Role of Mining in the Economic Development of Idaho Territory." *Oregon Historical Quarterly* 59 (June 1958): 116–51.

Boner, Harold A. *The Giant's Ladder: David H. Moffat and his Railroad*. Milwaukee: Kalmbach Publishing Co., 1962.

Bonfils, Winifred Black. *The Life and Personality of Phoebe Apperson Hearst*. San Francisco: John Henry Nash, 1928.

Burdette, Robert J., ed. *American Biography and Genealogy: California Edition*. 2 vols. Chicago: Lewis Publishing Co., 1912.

Burkhart, J. A. "The Frontier Merchant and Social History." *Montana Magazine of History* 2 (October 1952): 5–15.

Byers, William N. *Encyclopedia of Biography of Colorado*. Chicago: Century Publishing and Engraving Co., 1901.

Cash, Joseph H. *Working the Homestake*. Ames: Iowa State University Press, 1973.

Chandler, Alfred D., Jr. "The Beginnings of 'Big Business' in American Industry." *Business History Review* 33 (Spring 1959): 1–31.

———. *Strategy and Structure, Chapters in the History of Industrial Enterprise*. Garden City, New York: Doubleday and Co., 1966. Originally published, 1962.

Coleman, Peter J. "Restless Grant County: Americans on the Move." *Wisconsin Magazine of History* 96 (Autumn 1962): 16–20.

Conlin, Joseph R. *Big Bill Haywood and the Radical Union Movement*. Syracuse. N.Y.: Syracuse University Press, 1969.

Curti, Merle. *The Making of an American Community: A Case Study of Democracy in a Frontier County*. Stanford, Calif.: Stanford University Press, 1959.

Dana, Julian. *The Man Who Built San Francisco: A Study of Ralston's Journey with Banners*. New York: Macmillan Co., 1936.

Davis, Samuel P., ed. *The History of Nevada*. 2 vols. Reno, Nev.: Elms Publishing Co., 1913.

Degler, Carl N. *The Age of the Economic Revolution, 1876–1900*. Glenview, Ill.: Scott, Foresman and Co., 1967.

Dubofsky, Melvyn. "The Leadville Strike of 1896–1897: An Appraisal." *Mid-America* 48 (April 1966): 99–118.

———. "The Origins of Western Working Class Radicalism, 1890–1905." *Labor History* 7 (Spring 1966): 131–54.

———. *We Shall Be All: A History of the Industrial Workers of the World*. Chicago: Quadrangle Books, 1969.

Ellsworth, Alonzo E. "Early Denver Business." *Denver Westerners Brand Book* 6 (1950): 243–62.

Fell, James E., Jr. "Nathaniel P. Hill, a Scientist-Entrepreneur in Colorado." *Arizona and the West* 15 (Winter 1973): 315–32.

Forbes, B. C. *Men Who Are Making America*. New York: B.C. Forbes Publishing Co., 1922.

Gandy, Lewis C. *The Tabors: A Footnote of Western History*. New York: Press of the Pioneers, 1934.

Garraty, John A. *The New Commonwealth, 1877–1890*. New York: Harper and Row, 1968.

Glasscock, C. B. *The War of the Copper Kings, the Builders of Butte and the Wolves of Wall Street*. New York: Grosset and Dunlap, 1966. Originally published, 1935.

Grant, Charles S. *Democracy in the Connecticut Frontier Town of Kent*. New York: Columbia University Press, 1961.

Greever, William S. *The Bonanza West: The Story of the Western Mining Rushes, 1848–1900*. Norman: University of Oklahoma Press, 1963.

Gregory, Frances W., and Neu, Irene D. "The American Industrial Elite in the 1870s, Their Social Origins." In *Men in Business: Essays in the History of Entrepreneurship*, edited by William Miller, pp. 193–211. Cambridge, Mass.: Harvard University Press, 1952.

Griswold, Don L., and Jean H. *The Carbonate Camp Called Leadville*. Denver: University of Denver Press, 1951.

Hale, Jesse D. "The First Successful Smelter in Colorado." *Colorado Magazine* 13 (September 1936): 161–67.

Hansen, Gary B. "Industry of Destiny: Copper in Utah." *Utah Historical Quarterly* 31 (Summer 1963): 262–79.

Henretta, James A. "Economic Development and Social Structure in Colonial Boston." *William and Mary Quarterly* 22 (January 1965): 75–92.

Holbrook, Stewart H. *The Rocky Mountain Revolution*. New York: Henry Holt and Co., 1956.

Hoyt, Edwin P. *The Guggenheims and the American Dream*. New York: Funk and Wagnalls, 1967.

Irvine, Leigh H., ed. *A History of the New California, Its Resources and People*. 2 vols. New York: Lewis Publishing Co., 1905.

Jackson, W. Turrentine. *Treasure Hill, Portrait of a Silver Mining Camp*. Tucson: University of Arizona Press, 1963.

Jensen, Vernon H. *Heritage of Conflict: Labor Relations in the Nonferrous Metals Industry up to 1930*. Ithaca, N.Y.: Cornell University Press, 1950.

Johnson, Allen; Malone, Dumas; and et al, eds. *Dictionary of American Biography*. 22 vols. and supplements. New York: Charles Scribner's Sons, 1928–58.

Kneiss, Gilbert H. *Bonanza Railroads*. Stanford, Calif.: Stanford University Press, 1941.

Knight, Jesse William. *The Jesse Knight Family: Jesse Knight, His Forebears and Family*. Salt Lake City: Deseret News Press, 1940.

Lavender, David. *Nothing Seemed Impossible: William C. Ralston and Early San Francisco*. Palo Alto, Calif.: American West Publishing Co., 1975.

———. *The Rockies*. New York: Harper and Row, 1968.

Leipheimer, E. G. *The First National Bank of Butte, Seventy-Five Years of Continuous Banking Operation 1877 to 1952 under the Successive Ownership and Management of Three Men Each Named*

Andrew Jackson Davis. Butte, Mont.: First National Bank of Butte, 1952.

Lemon, James T., and Nash, Gary B. "The Distribution of Wealth in Eighteenth-Century America: A Century of Change in Chester County, Pennsylvania, 1693–1802." *Journal of Social History* 2 (Fall 1968): 1–24.

Lewis, Oscar. *Silver Kings: The Lives and Times of Mackay, Fair, Flood, and O'Brien, Lords of the Nevada Comstock Lode.* New York: Alfred A. Knopf, 1967. Originally published, 1947.

Lingenfelter, Richard E. *The Hardrock Miners: A History of the Mining Labor Movement in the American West, 1863–1893.* Berkeley: University of California Press, 1974.

Livingston-Little, D. E. "An Economic History of North Idaho—Discovery and Development of the Coeur d'Alene Mines." P. 5. *Journal of the West* 3 (July 1964): 318–54.

Lockridge, Kenneth A. *A New England Town, the First Hundred Years: Dedham, Massachusetts, 1636–1736.* New York: W. W. Norton and Co., 1970.

Mangam, William D. *The Clarks, an American Phenomenon.* New York: Silver Bow Press, 1941.

Mann, Ralph. "The Decade after the Gold Rush: Social Structure in Grass Valley and Nevada City, California, 1850–1860." *Pacific Historical Review* 41 (November 1972): 484–504.

Manning, Thomas G. *Government in Science: The U.S. Geological Survey, 1867–1894.* Lexington: University of Kentucky Press, 1967.

Manter, Ethel. *Rocket of the Comstock, The Story of John William Mackay.* Caldwell, Ida.: Caxton Printers, 1950.

Marcosson, Isaac F. *Metal Magic: The Story of the American Smelting and Refining Company.* New York: Farrar, Straus, and Co., 1949.

McMechen, Edgar C. *The Moffat Tunnel of Colorado: An Epic of Empire.* 2 vols. Denver: Wahlgreen Publishing Co., 1927.

Miller, Stuart C. *The Unwelcome Immigrant: The American Image of the Chinese, 1785–1882.* Berkeley: University of California Press, 1969.

Miller, William. "American Historians and the Business Elite." *Journal of Economic History* 9 (November 1949): 184–208.

Mills, C. Wright. "The American Business Elite: A Collective Portrait." *Journal of Economic History* (special issue *The Tasks of Economic History*) 5 (December 1945): 20–44.

Monaghan, Jay. *Chile, Peru, and the California Gold Rush of 1849.* Berkeley: University of California Press, 1973.

Nasatir, Abraham P. *The French in the California Gold Rush.* New York: American Society of the French Legion of Honor, 1934.

National Cyclopedia of American Biography. 51 vols. New York: James T. White and Co., 1892–1969.

Older, Fremont, and Cora. *George Hearst, California Pioneer.* Los Angeles: Westernlore Press, 1966. Originally published, 1933.

Ostrander, Gilman M. *Nevada, the Great Rotten Borough, 1859–1964.* New York: Alfred A. Knopf, 1966.

Parker, Watson. "The Causes of American Gold Rushes." *North Dakota History: Journal of the Northern Plains* 36 (Fall 1969): 337–45.

Paul, Rodman W. *Mining Frontiers of the Far West, 1848–1880.* New York: Holt, Rinehart and Winston, 1963.

Perez-Venero, Alejandro. "The 'Forty-Niners through Panama." *Journal of the West* 11 (July 1972): 460–69.

Peterson, Richard H. *Manifest Destiny in the Mines: A Cultural Interpretation of Anti-Mexican Nativism in California, 1848–1853.* San Francisco: R and E Research Associates, 1975.

Pitt, Leonard. "The Beginnings of Nativism in California." *Pacific Historical Review* 30 (February 1961): 23–38.

Pomeroy, Earl S. *The Territories and the United States, 1861–1890: Studies in Colonial Administration.* Philadelphia: University of Pennsylvania Press, 1947.

Quiett, Glenn C. *They Built the West: An Epic of Rails and Cities.* New York: Cooper Square Publishers, 1965. Originally published, 1934.

Rastall, Benjamin M. *The Labor History of the Cripple Creek District: A Study in Industrial Evolution.* Economic and Political Series, vol. 3, no. 1. Madison: University of Wisconsin Press, 1908.

Rayback, Joseph G. *A History of American Labor.* New York: Free Press, 1966.

Reavis, William A. "The Maryland Gentry and Social Mobility, 1637–1676." *William and Mary Quarterly* 14 (July 1957): 418–28.

Rickard, Thomas A. *A History of American Mining.* New York: American Institute of Mining Engineers, 1932.

Robbins, William G. "Opportunity and Persistence in the Pacific Northwest: a Quantitative Study of Early Roseburg, Oregon." *Pacific Historical Review* 39 (August 1970): 279–96.

Roberson, Nancy C. "Social Mobility in Ante-Bellum Alabama." *Alabama Review* 13 (April 1960): 135–45.

Shoebotham, H. Minar. *Anaconda, Life of Marcus Daly, the Copper King.* Harrisburg, Pennsylvania: Stackpole Co., 1956.

Smiley, Jerome C. *History of Denver, with Outlines of the Earlier*

History of the Rocky Mountain Country. Denver: J. H. Williamson and Co., 1903. Originally published, 1901.

Smith, Duane A. *Horace Tabor, His Life and the Legend*. Boulder: Colorado Associated University Press, 1973.

Smith, Robert W. *The Coeur d'Alene Mining War of 1892: A Case Study of an Industrial Dispute*. Corvallis: Oregon State University Press, 1961.

Spence, Clark C. *British Investments and the American Mining Frontier, 1860–1901*. Ithaca, N.Y.: Cornell University Press, 1958.

————. *Mining Engineers and the American West: The Lace-Boot Brigade, 1849–1933*. New Haven, Conn.: Yale University Press, 1970.

————. "The Mining Engineers in the West." In *The American West, an Appraisal*, edited by Robert G. Ferris, pp. 100–111. Santa Fe: Museum of New Mexico Press, 1963.

Sprague, Marshall. *Money Mountain: The Story of Cripple Creek Gold*. Boston: Little, Brown and Co., 1953.

Stewart, Robert E., Jr., and Mary F. *Adolph Sutro, a Biography*. Berkeley, Calif.: Howell-North, 1962.

Strassmann, W. Paul. *Risk and Technological Innovation: American Manufacturing Methods during the Nineteenth Century*. Ithaca, New York: Cornell University Press, 1959.

Thernstrom, Stephan. *The Other Bostonians: Poverty and Progress in the American Metropolis, 1880–1970*. Cambridge, Mass.: Harvard University Press, 1973.

————. *Poverty and Progress: Social Mobility in a Nineteenth Century City*. Cambridge, Mass.: Harvard University Press, 1964.

Tilton, Cecil G. *William Chapman Ralston, Courageous Builder*. Boston: Christopher Publishing House, 1935.

Turner, Frederick Jackson. *The Frontier in American History*. New York: Henry Holt and Co., 1920.

Waters, Frank J. *Midas of the Rockies*. Denver: Alan Swallow, 1949. Originally published, 1937.

Who Was Who in America, 1897–1942. vol. 1. Chicago: A. N. Marquis Co., 1943.

Who Was Who in America. Historical Volume, 1607–1896. rev. ed. Chicago: A. N. Marquis Co., 1967.

Wolle, Muriel S. *Stampede to Timberline: The Ghost Towns and Mining Camps of Colorado*. Denver: Sage Books, 1949.

Wyman, Mark. "Industrial Revolution in the West: Hard-Rock Miners and the New Technology." *Western Historical Quarterly* 5 (January 1974): 39–57.

INDEX